Customizable Security: Building Your Ideal Intrusion Detection System

Sanobar

Contents

Chapter 1

Introduction

The main goal of this book is to implement a scalable IDPS with a modular architecture, capable of uncovering unknown attack vectors and of sharing information between running instances.

Using Briareos [1] as a starting point for our system, we intend to improve its packet analysis performance, so as to reduce the resource usage on its host; implement a manager server, to ease the administration of multiple instances at once and provide the distributed system with retroactive attack prevention, in addition to detection.

JBriareos is a Java-written, host-based, scalable and modular IDPS, capable of both analysing network traffic and its host's behaviour to detect attack vectors. By performing these actions, this system is capable of dynamically creating new rules to detect and, more importantly, prevent malicious actions taken against its host. Furthermore, its users are able to create their own attack detection and prevention modules and processing pipelines, effectively being able to create a custom-built IDPS that suits their specific use case. As with most IDPSs, it is possible to increase the level of security provided by JBriareos, at the cost of decreasing the host's performance, by, for example, adding more modules to a single processing pipeline, or simply adding more processing pipelines overall. Hosts running a JHC instance are capable of protecting each other through the use of a manager server that propagates iptables rules created during the analysis of network traffic. This manager also allows hosts to fetch processing pipelines configurations, which can be maintained centrally on it, making it easier to manage a network containing various JHCs. Computationally intensive tasks such as performing data mining operations over the packets of a large network are also possible to be performed, by making use of its elastic distributed system, in which a host sends a task to a broker, which is responsible for distributing the workload between clusters of workers, that can be initialized or terminated, as the workload increases or decreases, respectively. These workers are also capable of communicating newly created iptables rules to the manager server, therefore propagating them to the host components, allowing the system the possibility to prevent further attacks, after one is uncovered, instead of simply detecting and logging it.

Chapter 2

State of the Art

2.1 Intrusion Detection and Prevention Systems

Intrusion detection and prevention systems, or IDPSs, are systems capable of protecting a single host or network by monitoring the behaviour of the host and/or the traffic of the network it may be deployed in. These systems' goal is to detect malicious activities in the system to be protected and proactively take action to prevent these activities from succeeding, as opposed to an intrusion detection system, or IDS, which simply logs the existence of such activities, doing nothing to stop them.

IDPSs can be network or host-based (NIDPS and HIDPS, respectively), which represents how and where the system mainly operates in order to fulfill its required goal. NIDPSs mainly work by analysing the entire network to achieve their goal, while HIDPSs monitor and analyse events occurring in the host running it. It is worthwhile to note that HIDPSs may be able to analyse network traffic as it arrives or exits the protected host, but a NIDPS does not have the ability to analyse a host's behaviour, such as what applications are being used or what files are being accessed, after having analysed the network's traffic.

2.1.1 Snort

Snort is a C-written, open-source NIDPS, capable of performing real-time traffic analysis and packet logging on IP networks by utilizing a rule-based system[2][3]. It was created in 1998 by Martin Roesch and acquired in 2013 by Cisco.

Snort allows users to create their own rules, but also provides a subscription-based service in which customers are given access to the latest rules and filters, improving the security offered by it and making it easier to use and manage.

Snort's architecture has four main parts: packet sniffing; packet preprocessing; intrusion detection and prevention and alerting and logging [4].

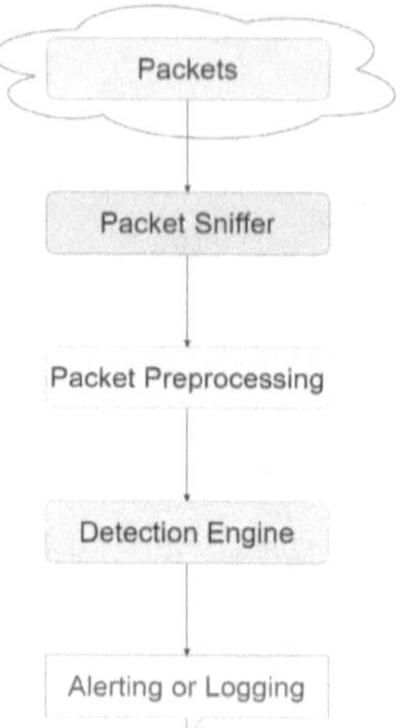

Figure 2.1: High level view of Snort's architecture

It is possible for Snort to function on three different modes: Sniffer mode, which simply displays on screen the captured packets; Packet Logger mode, which logs the captured packets to disk and the NIDS mode, which performs detection and analysis on the network traffic [5]. Although intrusion prevention is not one of its default modes, it is possible to enable it by using Snort in conjunction with either NFQueues or the DAQ, which take action after Snort detects an anomaly [6] [7].

The DAQ, or Data Acquisition library, is used by Snort for packet I/O operations. It is an abstraction layer that replaces direct libpcap function calls in order to facilitate cross-platform usage [8].

It is also worthwhile to mention that Snort's rules support and can trigger actions such as alerting and logging, as mentioned previously, but also packet drops and rejects.

Multithreading is only supported since Snort 3 [9], although it is possible to run multiple single instances of previous versions of Snort over multiple cores or threads, all feeding into the same log [10].

2.1.2   Suricata

Suricata is a C and Rust-written open-source NIDPS capable of real time intrusion detection and prevention, network security monitoring (NSM) and offline packet capture, or pcap, processing [11], developed by the Open Information Security Foundation, or OISF. Its first stable release was launched in July 2010.

It utilizes rule and signature-based methods to inspect a network's traffic and also supports Lua scripting, which improves its capability for detecting complex attack vectors. Suricata is also capable of detecting anomalies in the traffic it inspects.

Using Suricata, it is also possible to extract files from a HTTP session for posterior analysis, using its inbuilt HTTP engine [10] [12]. This engine possesses a stateful HTTP parser, built on libhtp, a security-aware parser for the HTTP protocol, developed by OISF until 2010 and then by Qualys [13], and it records per-server settings [14].

Other interesting features present in Suricata are, in example, the ability to perform actions (such as logging and storing) on SSL certificates and to implement IP reputation [14] [15].

Suricata's architecture has four main parts: packet acquisition; packet decoding; the detection pipeline and the output.

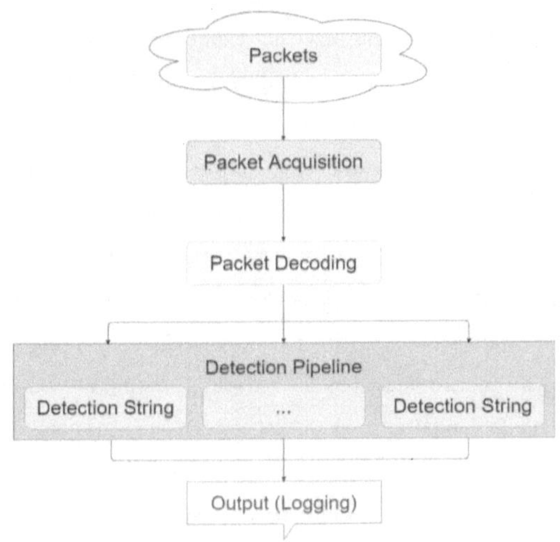

Figure 2.2: High level view of Suricata's architecture, based on [4]

Note that while Snort separates the packet sniffer and preprocessing layers of its architecture so that it is able to quickly identify the traffic stream and apply the correct rules to it, Suricata's architecture combines these two parts when acquiring new packets. It also contains a separate decoding function, which allows it to inspect the data stream at the application layer. Another difference is that Suricata allows for a chain of detection strings in a single pipeline [4].

Just like Snort, Suricata can be transformed into an IPS by utilizing its regular detection pipelines in conjunction with NFQueues; the AF_PACKET capture mode or NETMAPS [14] [16].

The support for multithreading and hardware acceleration are also important features of Suricata, as they allow for higher throughput and quicker packet inspections, specially on networks with a high traffic volume [15].

2.1.3   Zeek / Bro IDS

Zeek, until late 2018 known as Bro, is an open-source network analysis and security monitoring framework which can be used to create a NIDS with some layers of real time analysis of network events, that provides an extensive set of log files that record a network's activity in high-level terms [17]. It was created in 1995 by Vern Paxton and it is now being maintained and developed at the International Computer Science Institute, or ICSI, and the National Center for Supercomputing Applications, or NCSA, at Illinois, United States [18].

Zeek is a traffic analyser which uses deep packet inspection, or DPI, to detect intrusions in the network's traffic. It is also capable of performing tasks not related to security, such as traffic baselining and network performance tests, always maintaining an extensive application-layer state of the network it is deployed in. Zeek also allows users to write their own scripts using the domain-specific, Turing-complete Zeek scripting language and is able to be integrated with other applications for real-time sharing of information [18]. It also does not rely on a single detection method, using both signature-based detection modules and behavioral analysis.

Zeek logs information not only from every connection detected, but also from some application layer transcripts, such as, in example, HTTP sessions; DNS requests and replies and SSL certificates. In addition to logging, Zeek also provides its users with tools for analysis and detection tasks; HTTP session file extraction; software vulnerability reports and SSL certificate chains validation, which makes it a very powerful and flexible framework for managing the security of a network [17].

Zeek captures IP packets using the pcap library and transfers them to an event handler engine which accepts or rejects them, with the accepted packets being forwarded to the policy script interpreter. The event engine analyses live or recorded network traffic and generates events which can be anything from the initialization of Zeek to the analysis of a file that is travelling on the network or the acknowledgment of a new TCP connection. Events are policy neutral in that they are not good or bad but simply an "heads-up", notifying that something, which may or may not be later treated by a script, has happened. Events are handled by policy scripts, which analyse them to create action policies. The handling of events can be anything from simply logging it to taking an action such as executing a system command or executing another Zeek script [19].

Most of Zeek's analysers are located in its event engine with an accompanying policy script, which can be customized by the user. The analysers perform application layer decoding, anomaly detection, signature matching and connection analysis [20].

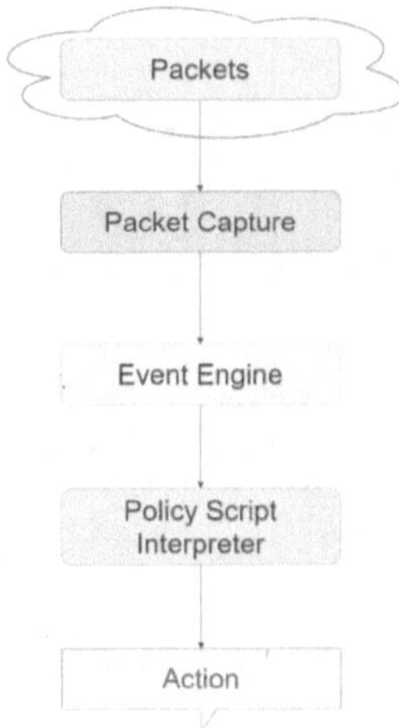

Figure 2.3: High level view of Zeek's architecture

One thing worth mentioning is that Zeek itself, in contrary to both Snort and Suricata, is a passive network traffic analyser, which means that despite being able to detect possible attacks and network malfunctions, it does nothing to prevent them from happening, although it is possible to activate responses to such events through the use of scripts which would be run by the policy script interpreter. For example, if Zeek logs an event that is attack/malfunction (something that Zeek itself does not know since events are neutral, as previously mentioned), there could be a policy script that handles that event by responding to the specific attack/malfunction occurring [19].

As Zeek is not multithreaded, to support high-performance environments, it is possible to create a "Zeek Cluster", in which a high-speed frontend machine acts as a load-balancer and appropriately distributes traffic across a number of backend machines running Zeek. A central manager system should coordinate the process, synchronizing state across the backends and providing the operators with a central management interface for configuration and access to aggregated logs [17]. Such clusters can be created using Zeek's integrated management framework, ZeekControl.

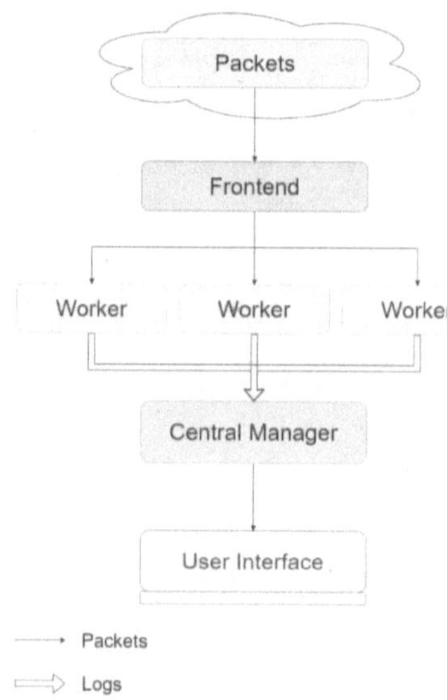

Figure 2.4: High level view of a Zeek Cluster's architecture

2.1.4 OSSEC

OSSEC, meaning Open Source HIDS SECurity, is a C-written open-source HIDS capable of performing real-time log analysis; file integrity verification and monitoring; rootkit and other malware detection, amongst others. It is also capable of providing active responses through firewall rules and/or third-party tool integration to problems it finds [21]. OSSEC was created by Daniel B. Cid and it is now managed by Atomicorp [22]. Atomicorp also makes available its own paid, OSSEC-based HIDS, named Atomic Enterprise OSSEC, which complements the former by providing a graphical user interface, making it more user friendly; active response management; a log and alert broker; threat intelligence, and other features that the open-source version does not [22].

OSSEC's architecture follows a simple worker-manager pattern. An agent runs on the hosts to be protected, collecting real-time information about the system and forwarding it to a manager. The manager, on the other hand, exists as a mean to centralize the logs of all the machines on a certain network, and to simplify their management. It stores the file integrity checking databases, the logs, events, and system auditing entries, as well as all the rules, decoders, and major configuration options of the agents [23]. This is a very important feature since if a host becomes compromised, by default, so does a HIDS running on it. As such, by offloading the logs to the manager, it is possible to avoid that information being compromised and tampered, hampering an administrator's ability to perceive if a system is malfunctioning. Also, all the communications between the agents and the manager are encrypted.

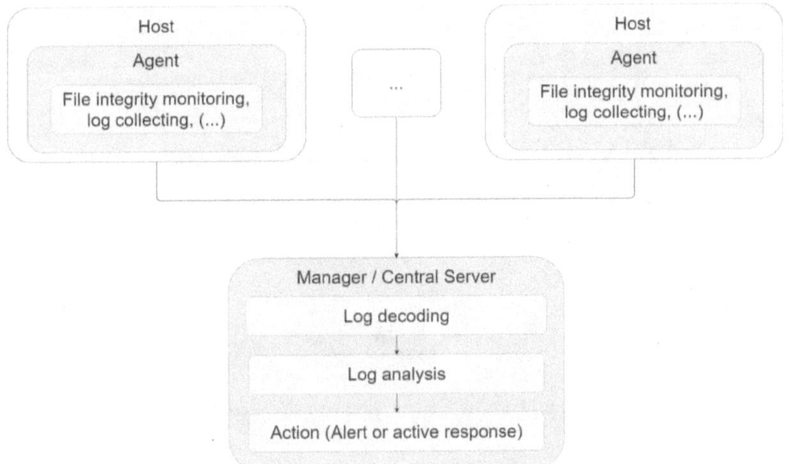

Figure 2.5: High level view of OSSEC's architecture

2.1.5 Open-source Tripwire

Open Source Tripwire is an open-source security and data integrity tool for monitoring and alerting on filesystem changes. It was created based on code originally contributed by Tripwire, Inc. in 2000.

A Tripwire integrity check compares the current filesystem state against a known baseline state, which is previously defined by the user via a policy file which specifies what resources and which of their attributes to monitor, and alerts on any changes it detects. The possible monitored attributes can be, for example, hashes, permissions and ownership, date of change, etc [24]. Both the baseline state and the policy file can be updated for example when an expected change occurs or to include new packages or filesystem resources.

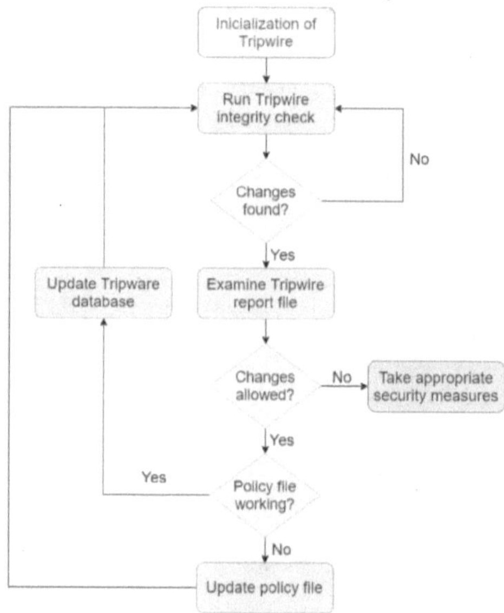

Figure 2.6: Tripwire's execution flowchart, based on [25]

2.1.6 Comparisons

	Snort	Suricata	Zeek	OSSEC	Tripwire	JBriareos
Programming Language	C	C and Rust	C++	C	C++ and Perl	Java
System Type	Network	Network	Network[1]	Host	Host	Host
Attack Detection	Yes	Yes	Yes	Yes	Yes	Yes
Attack Prevention	Yes	Yes	Yes[2]	Yes[3]	No	Yes
Multithreading	Yes[4]	Yes	No	No	No	Yes[5]
Task Offloading or Load Balancing	No	No	Yes[6]	No	No	Yes

[1] Zeek is a framework that can be used to create a NIDS.

[2] Through the use of policy scripts, which trigger actions.

[3] Through the use of firewall rules or third-party tool integration.

[4] From version 3 onward.

[5] One thread per processing pipeline, but multiple pipelines can be active.

[6] Using Zeek Clusters.

2.1.7 Comparing host and network-based IDSs

When it comes to intrusion detection, both solutions are viable, and the usage of one over the other depends on the conditions of the environment to be protected.

NIDSs usually use less resources than HIDSs, as they do not need to be deployed on every machine on the network, although, with a high enough volume of network traffic, having multiple HIDSs may be more beneficial than a single NIDS. Also, NIDSs are able to protect non-computer devices, such as firewalls, printers and routers and protection against bandwidth floods and denial of service attacks. A disadvantage of NIDSs over HIDSs are that NIDSs are single points of failure, as in if an attack passes through one, it may affect all "protected" hosts.

Only HIDSs can perform filesystem checking and monitoring, as NIDSs do not have access to the hosts they are protecting. Also, some HIDSs are able to analyse incoming and outgoing network traffic from the host they are deployed in, essentially simulating a NIDS dedicated to a single machine.

The best solution is to utilize both NIDSs and HIDSs to protect a network, as they complement each other and strive towards the same goal, but this depends on the amount of resources available to be spent on security, as having both NIDSs and HIDSs can be very costly.

2.2 Firewall rules management and distribution

2.2.1 Ansible

Ansible is an open-source tool that automates the management and deployment of configurations and applications, which allows for a better scaling and control over the infrastructure [26] [27].

Ansible users can define an inventory, which is essencially a list of hosts, and create and configure playbooks in order to execute actions on the former. These playbooks are ordered collections of tasks, which run modules or trigger handlers. These modules define commands to be executed. Playbooks are written in YAML, which makes them simple to use and read.

One of Ansible's many capabilities is to configure firewall and iptables rules, through the use of the `firewalld` [28] or the `iptables` [29] modules, respectively, and the extensive amount of operations and options which Ansible allows makes it a very powerful and flexible tool to do precisely that. In the case of iptables rules management, users can block IP address, redirect ports, accept or reject connections, flush filters and tables and much more.

2.2.2 Open-source Puppet

Puppet is yet another configuration and application management and deployment tool.

With Puppet, users define the desired end-state of the systems to be managed using a domain-specific language named Puppet Code. Puppet follows an agent-server architecture, in which the server stores the aforementioned desired end-state, and the agent translates that state into commands, and makes sure that the host it is deployed is kept in that condition [30].

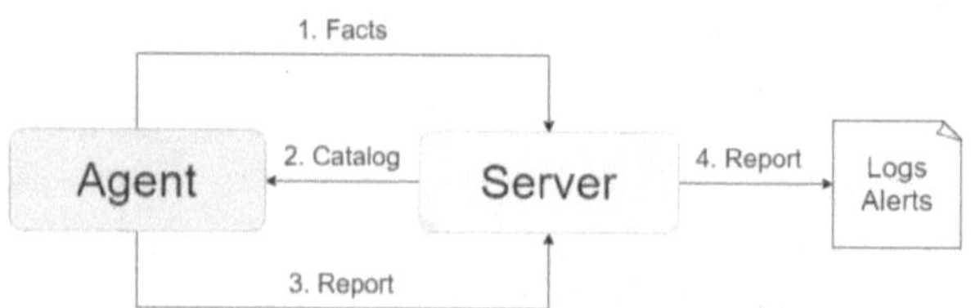

Figure 2.7: Puppet's architecture, based on [30]

As with Ansible, Puppet users can also manage iptables configurations with modules - more specifically, PuppetLabs' firewall module [31].

2.2.3   Firewall Builder

Firewall Builder is an open-source graphical user interface application that enables the configuration and management of multiple firewalls at once. It was created by Vadim Kurland and Mike Horn.

Users can create objects - that are abstractions representing IP addresses or networks used to represent items which will be referenced in firewall rules - and policies containing firewall rules which can then be deployed to the hosts in question. Firewall Builder includes many pre-built firewall policies templates and objects, but users can also create custom-made ones.

Although the last official update of Firewall Builder was in April of 2013, it was recently forked and is being maintained and updated by Sirius Bakke, who in 2017 released version 5.3.7, with version 6.0 being right now in beta.

Chapter 3

Background Work

3.1 Distributed Systems

A distributed system is a collection of independent computers appears to its users as a single coherent system [32]. Components present in these systems can be any type of node that can connect to the network and communication between these components is done through the passing of messages [33] [34].

Although, to a user, appearing as a single unit, distributed systems have much higher performance than their regular counterparts, as they utilize the resources of various interconnected machines to achieve their designated goals. By communicating through messages, the components of a distributed system do not need to share memory to access necessary data.

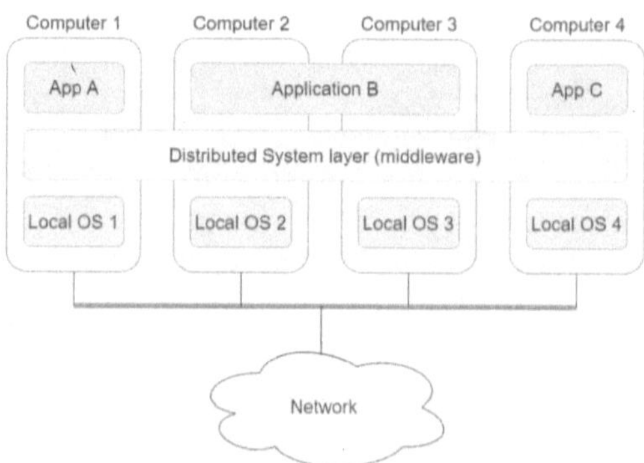

Figure 3.1: Example of a distributed system's architecture, based on [32]

Distributed systems are also highly scalable, as doing it is to simply add another machine to the already existing system, and provide great availability, as a malfunctioning machine usually does not impede the system from continuing its service, although at reduced performance, as the resources made available by that machine would no longer be used.

Middleware used to pass information in-between the components of a distributed system can be grouped into three categories: Remote Procedure Call (RPC), Object Request Broker (ORB) or Message-oriented Middleware (MOM). RPC-based middleware allows procedures in one application to call procedures in remote applications as if they were local calls. ORB-based middleware enable an application's objects to be distributed and shared across heterogeneous networks. MOM-based middleware allows distributed applications to communicate and exchange data by sending and receiving messages [35].

3.2 Message-oriented Middleware

MOM, as mentioned previously, is a category of middleware that allows the sharing of messages in-between applications.

Contrary to both RPC and ORB, which are synchronous messaging models that function partly as a bridge, locating the called procedure on a network and using network services to pass function or method parameters to the procedure and then to return results [35], MOM aims at asynchronous, fault-tolerant communication through the support of a messaging provider to mediate messaging operations. Instances send each other messages, which are queued, and senders do not need to wait for an immediate reply.

The main parts of a MOM system are the clients, messages, and the MOM provider, which includes an API to be used the a developer. The MOM provider uses different architectures to route and deliver messages: it can use a centralized message server or it can distribute routing and delivery functions to each client machine [35].

According to [36], there are three different types of receives supported by a message queue:

- A blocking receive, which will block until an appropriate message is available;

- A non-blocking receive, or a polling operation, which will check the status of the queue and return a message if available, or a not available indication otherwise;

- A notify operation, which will issue an event notification when a message is available in the associated queue.

Methods such as PUT, in which a message is inserted into a queue; GET, in which a message is fetched from a queue; POLL, which checks if a queue has pending messages and fetches the first if that is the case, and NOTIFY; which implements a mechanism that is triggered when a message is available in the queue, can be deduced from the definition of these receives.

3.3   ZeroMQ

ZeroMQ, or ZMQ, is a high-performance, asynchronous messaging library, focused at being used in distributed or concurrent applications [37]. It was created by iMatix, the designers behind the Advanced Message Queuing Protocol, or AMQP, in 2007.

Despite basically being a message-oriented middleware, ZMQ differs from them by not needing to possess a dedicated message broker. It is also very flexible, in that it supports common messaging patterns such as request/reply (or client/server); publisher/subscriber; and push/pull.

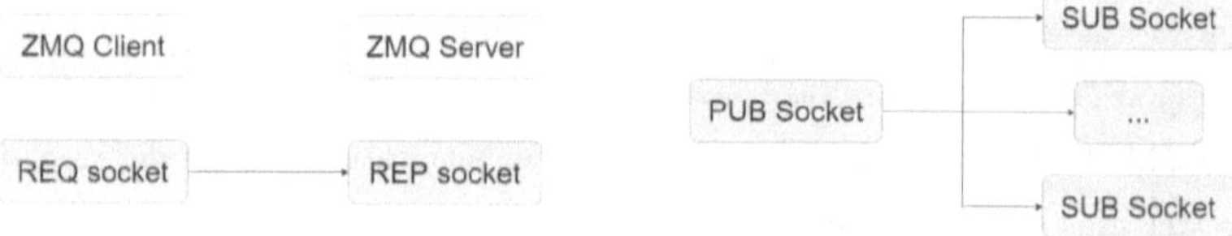

Figure 3.2: Example of request/reply (on the left) and publisher/subscriber (on the right) ZMQ sockets

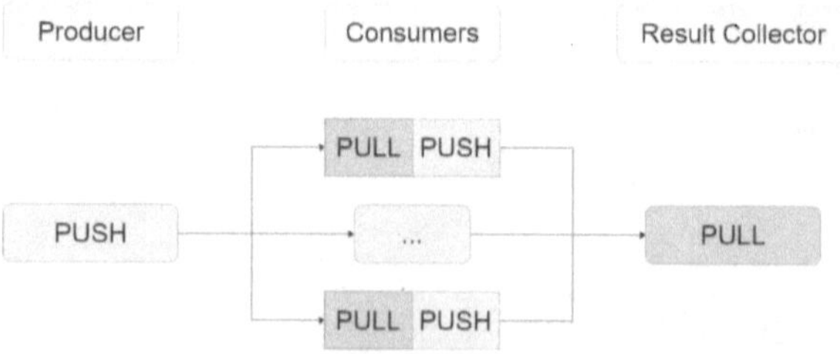

Figure 3.3: Example of push/pull socket connections, based on [38]

Libzmq, the low-level library behind ZMQ, is originally written in C++, but most common programming languages have bindings or native engines available. Also, ZMQ supports transport protocols such as TCP, UDP, inproc, gssapi and others, depending on the bindings/engine used. Message authentication and confidentiality is also possible, using the CURVE mechanism, which secures socket communications by utilizing elliptic curve-based encryption. This mechanism uses the CurveZMQ protocol, a protocol for secure messaging across the Internet, based on the CurveCP security handshake [39] [40] [41]. ZMQ certificates provide the public and secret key pair necessary for messaging with that mechanism [42].

The following example implements a JeroMQ [43] publisher/subscriber module, where the publisher (Listing 3.1) runs on the localhost, port 7777. In this case, the publisher sends a "Hello world!" string every five seconds to all its subscribers, which print it to the system output.

```java
1  ZContext context = new ZContext();
2  ZMQ.Socket publisher = context.createSocket(SocketType.PUB);
3
4  publisher.bind("tcp://localhost:7777");
5
6  while(True) {
7      try {
8          publisher.send("Hello world!");
9
10         Thread.sleep(5000);
11     } catch (Exception ignored) {}
12 }
```

Listing 3.1: JeroMQ publisher example

```java
1  ZContext context = new ZContext();
2  ZMQ.Socket subscriber = context.createSocket(SocketType.SUB);
3
4  subscriber.subscribe("");
5  subscriber.connect("tcp://localhost:7777");
6
7  while(True)
8      System.out.println(subscriber.recvStr());
```

Listing 3.2: JeroMQ subscriber example

Note that the subscriber (Listing 3.2), through the use of the `subscribe` method, has the possibility to subscribe to whatever is relevant to himself by setting the `ZMQ_SUBSCRIBE` option. This method establishes a message filter on the subscribe socket. In the above case, the subscriber chose to receive everything the publisher sends.

3.4 IDS performance comparison

According to Antonatos, Anagnostakis and Markatos [44], the two basic metrics for measuring an NIDS's performance are the attack detection rate and the amount of false positives. While these reflect the quality of NIDSs based on statistical anomaly detection methods, for content-matching systems such as Snort or Suricata, in which the detection process is much more exact, we should take into consideration the capacity of the system, as if all packets are able to be processed, then all the attacks specified in the rulesets will be detected. In other words, in content-matching systems, assuming a ruleset encompassing every known and unknown attack, only packets that are not analysed are able to pierce the system's defenses.

Mell et. al. [45] also list a set of measurements that can be made in order to evaluate an IDS: coverage (in other words, the amount of attacks possible to detect); probability of detection and of false alarm; attack resistance; ability to detect unknown attacks and to identify detected ones; and system and network capacity.

In both cases, capacity is a term that can be measured by encompassing metrics such as analysed packets, new connections and alarms/logs per second; and the amount of concurrent connections. The amount of analysed packets per second is the throughput of the system. By these metrics, in example, the higher the throughput of an IDS, the higher its capacity, and, therefore, the better its performance.

An example of the usage of these metrics when evaluating the performances of IDSs was done by Day and Burns [46], who compared the single-threaded Snort v2.8.5.2 with the multi-threaded Suricata v1.0.2, in February 2011.

Chapter 4

Briareos System

4.1 Capabilities, objectives and requirements

Briareos is a host-based intrusion detection and prevention system possessing a modular framework and a distributed system to which users can offload tasks. This system is capable of detecting and preventing both known and unknown intrusion attempts on its host by analysing the network traffic in conjunction with the operating system in which it is running. When detecting attacks, it is able to create local rules in order to prevent them from re-occurring. By being implementing with a modular framework, Briareos' users are able to adjust the system to its needs and requirements, being able to alter the amount of security offered, in exchange for system resources - as is the case for most IDSs. With its distributed system, users can offload packet analysis tasks to it, in order to spare a host's resources. This allows for a much thorougher analysis to be executed, without compromising the host's functioning.

4.2 Architecture and components

4.2.1 Modular Framework

When performing an analysis, Briareos runs a collection of modules, the execution order of which is detailed and encapsulated in pipelines. In other words, pipelines are ordered collections of modules which will perform some computation which was triggered by the capture of some network packet. The execution order of the modules contained in pipelines is described via a directed graph, an example of which is present in Figure 5.3 - although that figure pertains to the JBriareos system, it can also be applied to this specific part of Briareos.

Pipelines and their modules and configurations are loaded on a host component's startup, setting the environment for the analysis of the traffic which will be captured.

4.2.2 Host Component

A Briareos Host Component is responsible for capturing network traffic and analysing it. For that to be possible, it contains two main components: a network traffic interceptor and a network traffic processing engine.

This component's processing engine is capable of analysing traffic independently, either synchronously - also named the "inline" processing mode, in which the system waits for the analysis' result -, asynchronously - also named the "parallel" processing mode, in which case the opposite occurs -, or of sending analysis tasks to the previously mentioned distributed system - which is named the "distributed" processing mode. Of these three processing modes, the only one which is capable of independently preventing attacks is the "inline" mode, as the other two require a favorable pipeline configuration and some form of third-party intervention - in example, an administrator manually checking analysis results - before being able to do so. Otherwise, the latter two modes are only able to offer intrusion detection, but not prevention.

4.2.3 Distributed System

Briareos' distributed system was implemented so that users have the option of offloading analysis tasks to it, in order to reduce resource usage of the host component on the machine in which it is deployed.

This distributed system can be divided in three main parts: workers - which are the components of the system which perform the analysis tasks -, worker clusters - groups of workers formed in order to facilitate their management -, and a broker - which relays the tasks received from host components to workers of the system.

The broker also contains a worker manager, which is responsible for collecting usage metrics from each cluster's workers, and issuing directives to them to start of stop worker instances, depending on the data collected.

When distributing tasks among workers, the broker always relays them using a least-recently used algorithm, in which the worker that least-recently received an analysis task will be chosen for the next task received.

4.3   Shortcomings and limitations

1. Briareos was implemented in Python.

   Although Python is an accessible and flexible programming language and therefore a good choice in order to implement proof-of-concept projects, it lacks in a major key aspect: performance. An IDS should use the least possible amount of resources of the host, in order not to disrupt its usual functioning, which is why many of the more widespread and used IDS are implemented in efficient programming languages such as Rust, C or C++, as shown in Section 2.

2. Information about detected attacks is not propagated to different host component instances.

   Although being able to detect and prevent unknown attack vectors is a big advantage of Briareos over other systems, a Briareos host component is not able to share information about detected attacks with other running hosts. This makes it so that each and every running instance has to detect (and possibly prevent) the exact same attack before the whole network is immune, which obviously spends more system resources than would otherwise be needed, as each instance needs to run the same packet analysis.

3. The distributed system is capable of detecting attacks, but not of preventing them.

   The distributed system functions basically as a system which analyses packets received from the host components and logs the results of those tasks.

   If a host component lets a malicious packet through (without knowing it is such, as we are assuming that the analysis is being performed by the distributed system), and only after receives information an intrusion was detected, it may already be too late to reverse the attack. This scenario can be prevented by proper pipeline configuration on the hosts, but the distributed system itself is never capable of preventing attacks from occurring in the first place. Also, as with the host components, this system does not share information about detected attacks with running host component instances, so that they may protect themselves.

4. Information about attacks and intrusions is not shared.

   Although the idea of information sharing is present in Briareos' paper [1], it was not practically implemented. As such, each host component runs independently from each other, and the distributed system simply logs information about attacks detected itself has detected.

In our work, we tackled all of these issues by creating a new intrusion detection and prevention system that not only makes use of the capabilities and architecture of Briareos and upgrades them, but also implements new functionalities, features and components, as explained in the following chapters.

Chapter 5

Architecture

5.1 Architecture Overview

We implemented the overall, high-level architecture of our system similar to that of Briareos, with the addition of new features and functionalities we provide. In order to differentiate our contributions to those of Briareos, we will explicitly mention whenever we adapted parts of the former and compare components that we adjusted to be used within our system with those on which they were based.

JBriareos hosts are protected by the JBriareos Host Component, or JHC. Each host may receive and analyse network traffic, both incoming and outgoing, to decide if packets are accepted or dropped. Each JHC can be configured differently, with each instances' computations being decided by some processing pipelines. Processing pipelines will be explained in further detail in its own section, alongside the modules executed by them.

Unlike Briareos, which simply offers a host component and a distributed task offloading system, we provided an implementation of a manager server, which is used by the other components of the system to share information about iptables rules, processing pipelines and modules, so that that information does not need to be present in each host.

The JBriareos Distributed Offloading System's goal is to reduce the workload of the hosts. In exchange for that, the JDS simply provides the host with intrusion detection but not instantaneous attack prevention. The use of the JDS is optional, and its architecture and functioning will also be further detailed in its own section.

In Briareos there are three possible processing modes - inline, parallel, and distributed - whereas in JBriareos there are only two modes - inline and distributed. Taking into consideration the advantages and disadvantages of the parallel processing mode described in [1], practically in all of the use cases in which it could be used over the inline processing mode it is possible to simply use the distributed processing mode instead. Therefore, the parallel processing mode was discarded in JBriareos.

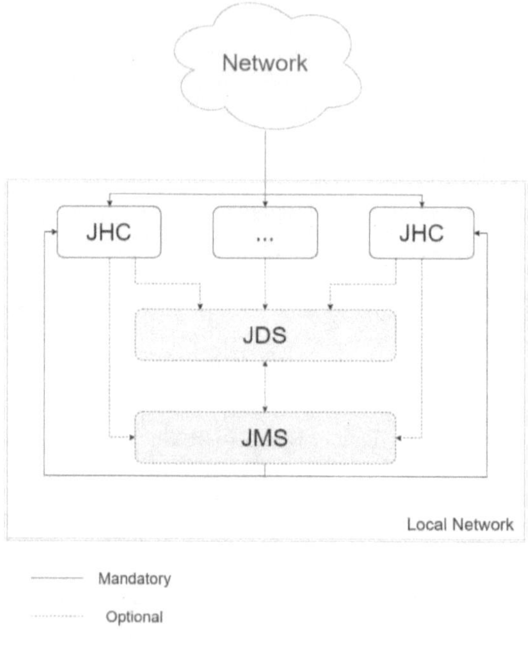

Figure 5.1: JBriareos' architecture

5.2   Host Component

The architecture of a JBriareos Host Component is similar to that of its Briareos counterpart in that it can be divided into two different main components: a network traffic interceptor and a processing engine, although in our system the engine is encapsulated inside the interceptor in order to simplify the structure of each individual component/class. The network interceptor is responsible for creating iptables rules that will capture network traffic, and for sending the captured packet to the engine for processing. The engine, as mentioned, is responsible for processing captured packets and acting upon them by issuing verdicts and creating new iptables rules to prevent attacks.

The requirements of a JBriareos Host Component, which are basically the same as in Briareos, are the following:

- Interception and analysis of incoming and outgoing traffic;

- Detection and prevention of known and unknown attack vectors;

- Traffic processing inline or forwarded to a distributed offloading system;

- Support for detection of intrusions at the OS level;

- Automatic intelligence sharing;

- Ability to receive and apply new iptables rules from a manager server.

5.2.1   Configurations and Loading Phase

All the configurations that a JHC needs to operate are provided locally in a JSON file which is loaded on each instance's startup. This file should contain the JDS broker's address, alongside information about the JMS's ZMQ sockets and the processing pipelines to be used by the processing engine. If connecting to the JMS, then its certificate must also be provided in its own file, otherwise meaningful connections from the JHC to the JMS will be denied by the latter, as sharing and fetching information with the JMS must be done in a secure fashion.

The loading phase of the JHC initializes the network traffic interceptor, the processing engine and the interfaces to communicate with both the distributed offloading system and the manager server.

Initially, if a host already possesses a ZMQ certificate for secure messaging, then it is reused. On the other hand, if a host does not have a ZMQ certificate generated, then it cannot connect to the JMS, and must rely on the local pipeline configurations. After confirming the existence of a ZMQ certificate, a JHC sends its certificate's ID to the JMS, for it to check if that certificate is present in the pool of accepted connections. If the JMS confirms that the certificate is accepted, then the JHC can perform further communications with the JMS, such as requesting iptables rules and pipeline configurations, all of which will be encrypted. On the flip side, if the certificate is not accepted by the JMS, the JHC will try to function using its own configurations, just as if it did not have any certificate. Iptables rules requested from the JMS would have been created manually by an administrator or automatically by the JBriareos system, when an attack or vulnerability was detected. An example of successful communications between a JHC and the JMS, during the loading phase, is shown in Figure 5.2.

5.2.1.1 Processing Engine

The processing engine creates the processing pipelines by loading the modules used by them, the information of which is received after an initial connection from the JHC to the JMS, in which the former asks the latter for the configurations to be used by a specific processing pipeline, as shown in Figure 5.2. Pipelines are executed sequentially by order of its load, which is specified in the JHC configuration file.

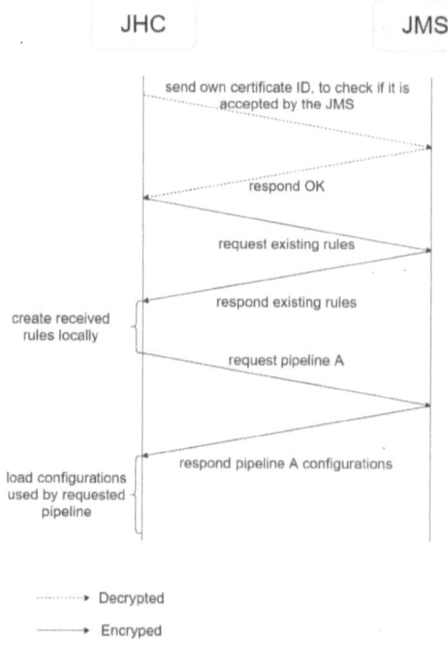

Figure 5.2: Loading phase JHC example

5.2.1.2 Processing Pipelines

A processing pipeline is essentially a directed graph with additional meta-information relating to the processing. Each node in the directed graph corresponds to a unique processing module, which can perform computations such as analysing and modifying the captured packet, seeing how it interacts with the system, and so forth. The idea of abstracting pipelines to what essentially are directed graphs was imported from Briareos, although the implementation of both pipelines and their processing modules was adapted to work with our system.

A pipeline contains the following information:

- Name: The pipeline's name;

- Port: The port that the pipeline is attached to;

- Protocol: Which transport protocol (UDP, TCP, etc.) the pipeline is processing. This protocol has to be accepted by JBriareos;

- Interface: The network interface that the pipeline is attached to;

- Type: "input" or "output", depending on which iptables chain the pipeline is attached to;

- Mode: "inline" or "distributed", depending on which processing mode the configuration specifies;

- Verdict: "accept" or "drop". The default verdict that the pipeline issues on a processed packet;

- Graph: A custom directed graph which specifies the execution order of the modules loaded by the pipeline. Each node of the graph represents a module.

The setting of these attributes can be done either in the pipeline configuration file, which is present in the JMS, or in the JHC configuration file.

If a JHC wants to fetch a pipeline's configuration from the JMS, then that pipeline's "name" attribute must be set in the former's configuration file. That attribute must match the file name in which that pipeline's configurations are defined. If there are attributes defined in both the JMS and the JHC, those defined in the JMS will be prioritised.

From all the attributes mentioned above, only the pipeline's name and modular structure, which is used to form the graph, have to be provided in the pipeline configuration file present in the JMS. Every other attribute is optional, either a default or null value being provided to the constructor in case it is not defined with the configuration files mentioned previously. In the JHC, assuming that it is fetching configurations from the JMS, only the pipeline file name has to be provided, otherwise, the pipeline's name and modular structure must be provided, just like in a configuration file present in the JMS. A port for the pipeline to be attached to must also be provided by either the JHC or the JMS. Examples of these configuration files will be provided in chapter 6 (Figure 6.6).

The pipeline cannot be cyclic, otherwise the execution would not terminate. Also, each node/module connection has to have the same "module output" into "next module input" type, otherwise the execution will fail.

5.2.1.3 Network Interceptor

To intercept network traffic, we utilize University of Parma's NEMO's nfqueue library Java bindings. The nfqueue library is an iptables and ip6tables target that delegates the decision on packets to a userspace software [47], and it was also used in the traffic capture operations performed by Briareos.

NEMO is an open-source Java-based network emulator created by the NetSec Research Group of the Department of Engineering and Architecture of the University of Parma. Utilizing NEMO's nfqueue bindings provides our system with the possibility to expand the protocols accepted by its processing pipelines and modules - IPv6, in addition to IPv4; arp, dhcp, icmp, etc. [48]

After the initial loading phase of the processing engine, in which the processing pipelines are created, the network interceptor creates iptables rules based on the attributes listed previously at 5.2.1.2. Each pipeline is matched with the nfqueue number of its created rule.

After the creation of the iptables rules, the network interceptor binds all queues to a custom made handler, which passes the received packet data and the nfqueue number to the processing engine, giving start to the processing phase.

The maximum number of nfqueues that can be present in a system at a certain given point is 2^{16}, or 65536, which should be a big enough number for any need it might have of them, given that there should not be that many open network services running at the same time in that same system.

5.2.2 Processing Phase

During the processing phase, a packet captured by the network interceptor is run through a pipeline's modules, which return a verdict on the packet. If no module issues an action on the captured packet, the pipeline's default verdict will be the one applied by the interceptor's handler. If the pipeline is executed in the "distributed" mode, in order words, if the packet is sent to the JDS for analysis, then even if the JDS's workers issue a verdict on the packet, it is simply disregarded by the handler, which utilizes the previously mentioned pipeline default verdict. This means that pipelines executed in "distributed" mode, as mentioned in section 5.1, only provide intrusion detection but not prevention, although they are able to retroactively prevent those same attacks, if a rule created by a worker of the JDS is shared to the JMS and propagated through the network.

Our solution, taking inspiration from Briareos, propagates the output of a module to its neighbours by utilizing a breadth-first search algorithm. The algorithm examplified in Listing 5.1 is a simplified version of the algorithm used to run packets through a pipeline. Initially, a `QueueObject` is added to a list (line 3). Those objects contain a node and the inputs that that node will receive. While there are objects in the list (line 4), we remove the first (line 5), get the associated node and inputs (lines 6-7) and run the packet through the node's module, receiving an output (line 8). If after the analysis the packet has a final verdict, we simply return it (lines 9-10), otherwise we add the neighbours of the current node and the generated output to the list, as a `QueueObject` (lines 12-13). In the end, when the queue is empty, we simply return the resulting packet (line 15).

```
1   BPacket process(BPacket packet) {
2       LinkedList<QObj> queue = new LinkedList<>;
3       queue.add(new QObj(pipelineGraph.rootNode, new ModuleIO()));
4       while(!queue.isEmpty()) {
5           QObj queueObject = queue.removeFirst();
6           Node node = queueObject.node;
7           ModuleIO input = queueObject.input;
8           ModuleIO output = node.process(packet, input);
9           if(packet.hasFinalVerdict())
10              return packet;
11
12          for (Node neighbour : node.getNeighbours())
13              queue.add(new QObj(neighbour, output));
14      }
15      return packet;
16  }
```

Listing 5.1: Packet processing algorithm example

Listing 5.1 is simply used here as an abstraction or as an explanation aid. The extended version of the algorithm receives a `byte[]` form of the captured packet and transforms it into a `BPacket` data structure and also handles cases in which a node has multiple incident nodes, instead of a single one, meaning it has multiple inputs.

Every packet has a verdict attached to it - initially equal to the pipeline's default verdict - that might change depending on the results of its analysis. This verdict is the value which will be used by the network interceptor to handle the packet. It is worthwhile to note that the handler can act upon the packet, even if the latter's verdict is not final. This means that there is no need for the pipeline to have a single "end node", like in Figure 5.3, as a verdict will be deduced from the packet's information after all the modules finish processing it. In example, assuming that in Figure 5.3, the nodes are processed alphabetically, then, if no final verdict is issued on a packet, that packet's verdict will be whatever the value is after node F, the last node to be executed.

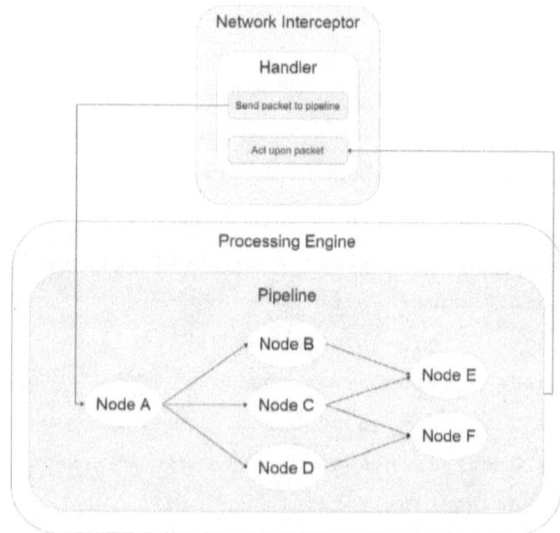

Figure 5.3: Pipeline execution example

5.2.3 Nodes / Modules

A node in the pipeline's graph represents a processing module. "Nodes" and "Modules" are interchangeable, therefore when one of these is referred, the other can be inferred.

Data structures named `BPackets`, which are further explained in Section 5.2.4, are passed through the nodes to be used for their processing. Nodes also always have to be provided with module-specific input and produce output, even though it may be empty.

A `ModuleIO` data structure should indicate the data type being used and the data itself. This is used to check if the input received by a module from the previous ones is the type of input it wants to receive. More information about this data structure will be provided in Section 6.2.3.

Any type of module can be created and inserted into a pipeline, as long as it abides by the rules set by the creation of the pipeline. Modules that function as system monitors and managers, attack detectors, incident handlers and many more can be developed by making use of the provided extensible JBriareos engine module class.

5.2.4 BPackets

`BPackets`, which are data structures that encapsulate captured packets and were imported and adapted from Briareos, and extended by us, were created so that users may easily utilize and create methods to access and/or modify a packet's fields. This data structure, contains useful information for the functioning of the processing pipelines and modules, such as the current packet's verdict and if it is final. In other words, `BPackets` contain the following information:

- Verdict: The current verdict of the pipeline which is analysing this `BPacket`;

- IsFinalVerdict: A boolean indicating if the `BPacket`'s current verdict is final. This can be set by a module's processing function and can be used to terminate the packet's processing before the end of the pipeline;

- Payload: The captured packet, in `byte[]` form;

- Packet: A reconstruction of the captured packet, utilizing NEMO's nfqueue bindings;

- Protocol: The captured packet's transport protocol. This is used as a helper in operations with the reconstructed packet, as different protocols have different ways of accessing data;

Every parameter except the `Payload` and the `Verdict` are initialized with default values. Users should be able choose either to utilize the raw data of the captured packet, present in `Payload`, or to reconstruct the packet and utilize the simpler `Packet` parameter. This differentiation is simply so that there is more flexibility when working with a captured packet's data.

5.3   Manager Server

The JBriareos Manager Server is the system component that is responsible for distributing processing pipeline configurations and iptables rules by the running instances. In other words, the JMS is the component that distributes information throughout the JBriareos network.

The pipeline configurations present in the JMS have the parameters that will have to be used by the instances requesting that pipeline. If some parameter is not present in the configuration that is in the JMS, that same parameter should be set in each instance, depending on whatever is needed. In example, if the processing mode ("inline" or "distributed", as mentioned in 5.2.1.2), is not set in the JMS, each instance can decide in its own configuration which of the processing modes it will use.

The JMS's iptables rules can be created manually in the machine or collected automatically from the JHCs and the JDS's workers through the use of push / pull ZMQ sockets, in case they are created and shared. This makes it so that in case a host detects an irregularity and creates an iptables rule to prevent it, all other running instances will be able to create that same rule in order to protect themselves as well, if connected to the JMS. These rules are stored in a file in the JMS so that new instances joining the network get updated with all the rules created so far, and passed to the hosts utilizing publisher / subscriber ZMQ sockets.

An example of the communications when a new instance joins the network can be viewed in Figure 5.2 and of the use of the JMS in the network in Figure 5.1.

5.4   Distributed Offloading System

As mentioned previously, the JDS's main purpose, is to reduce the workload of the JHCs by offloading the computation to clusters of workers, at the cost of simply providing detection and not instantaneous attack prevention. The JDS should be able to start and stop workers at will, depending on the workload of the workers running in each existing cluster. Our JDS was initially based on Briareos' BDS, but we improved some aspects of its performance and ease of operation, and we managed to provide it with the possibility of preventing intrusions and/or attacks through the use of the JMS to propagate analysis results, instead of simply logging them.

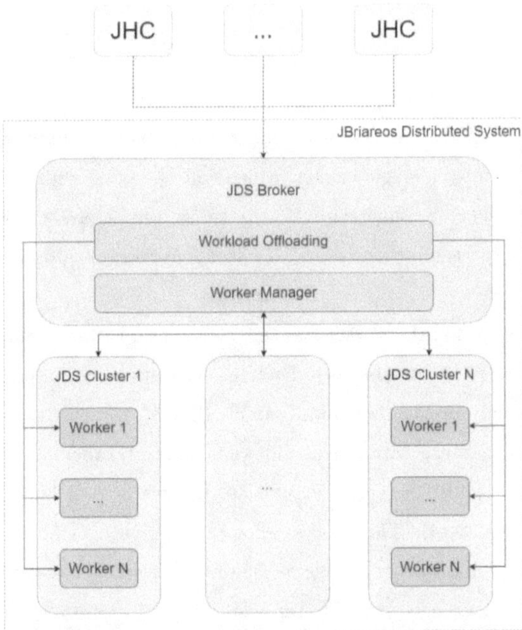

Figure 5.4: Architecture of the JDS

The JDS, just like Briareos' distributed system, can be divided into four main components, as shown in Figure 5.4: a broker; worker clusters; workers and a worker manager.

The workers are the components that perform a packet's analysis. They are Docker containers and should have access to be JMS, in order to be able to publish new rules, in case an attack is detected. This way, the first time an attack is detected it may not be prevented, depending on the pipeline's default verdict, but further attempts will be.

Clusters are machines that contain workers. They are in permanent contact with the worker manager, which collects usage metrics of workers present in the former. That information is then used to start or stop worker containers. When booted, a cluster rebuilds the workers' Docker image in order to provide them with the JMS's and the cluster's certificate so that they are able to request pipeline configurations from the JMS and publish newly created rules.

The worker manager is the part of the Broker that is responsible for collecting information about the various clusters and the workers running in them. It should be able to order a cluster to start or stop worker instances, depending on that cluster's performance metrics.

The broker is responsible for initializing the worker manager and for distributing the workload between the different Workers, after receiving data from a JHC instance. It records the status of TCP connections, similarly to a (very) simplified TCB, and maps an entire TCP stream to a single worker, which will be tasked with analysing all packets received from that specific connection. If a packet's transfer protocol is not TCP (UDP, for instance), or if the connection is new, it chooses Workers based on a LRU algorithm, as in Briareos.

The algorithms used in the worker manager's computation of the clusters' performance (Listings 5.2 and 5.3) are the same as in Briareos. In Listing 5.2, for each recorded worker statistics (line 4), and for each individual sample (line 5), we store the CPU and memory usage of statistics than are within a certain time interval, otherwise those statistics are discarded (lines 6-11). In the end, we calculate the averages of both the CPU and the memory usage (lines 13-14). This process allows us to create a sliding window algorithm for the average CPU and memory usage of the workers running, values which can then be analysed to find out when to start or stop workers. In Listing 5.3, we continuously run the sliding window algorithm to update the usage metrics (line 2), starting a new worker in the least used cluster, in case either average is above a certain threshold (lines 3-6), or stopping a worker in the most used cluster, in case a average is below a certain threshold, and the other is not too high (lines 7-10).

```
1   List cpu_values;
2   List mem_values;
3   Time current_time = getTime();
4   for (Stats stats : worker_stat_history) {
5       for (Stat stat : stats) {
6           if (current_time - stat.time <= metric_interval) {
7               cpu_values.add(stat.cpu);
8               mem_values.add(stat.mem);
9           }
10          else
11              stats.remove(stat)
12      }
13      average_cpu = average(cpu_values);
14      average_mem = average(mem_values);
```

15 }

<hr>

Listing 5.2: Worker manager's sliding window algorithm

<hr>

```
1  while (true) {
2      runSlidingWindowAlgorithm();
3      if (average_cpu >= CPU_UPPER_BOUND || average_mem >=
       MEM_UPPER_BOUND) {
4          Cluster cluster = getClusterWithLeastUsage();
5          cluster.createNewWorker();
6      }
7      else if ((average_cpu <= CPU_LOWER_BOUND && average_mem <
       MEM_UPPER_BOUND) || (average_mem <= MEM_LOWER_BOUND &&
       average_cpu < CPU_UPPER_BOUND)) {
8          Cluster cluster = getClusterWithMostUsage();
9          cluster.stopWorker();
10     }
11     sleep(interval);
12  }
```

<hr>

Listing 5.3: Worker manager's worker start/stop decision algorithm

The algorithm used in the broker's choice of worker to which the data will be sent, exemplified in Listing 5.4, is based on Briareos', but also takes into consideration the transport protocol used and the previously recorded connections. In this Listing, we continuously check for messages both from the backend (line 4) and the frontend (in case there are available workers; lines 9-10). In this example, messages from the backend are simply workers registering themselves on the broker (lines 5-6), but in the implemented algorithm, messages from the backend may also be results of packet analysis. In case there are available workers and messages from the frontend, we assume the received message is a packet (line 11), and we choose a worker to be tasked with that packet's analysis (lines 13-23). In that choice, we take into account if the packet is part of a TCP connection (line 13). If it is, but the connection is new, we simply choose the first available worker in the list (lines 14-15), otherwise we check in the TCB which worker was tasked with the analysis of packets from that same connection (lines 16-17). If the packet is not a part of a TCP stream, then we choose the first available worker (line 19). Finally, we offload the task to the chosen worker (lines 22-23). For parsimony's sake, the algorithm displayed in this Listing is a simplified version of the real algorithm, which is shown in Listing 6.22.

```
1  List availableWorkers;
2  MiniTCB tcb;
3  while true {
4      if has message from backend {
5          String workerId = backend.recv();
6          availableWorkers.addLast(workerId);
7      }
8
9      if availableWorkers is not empty {
10         if has message from frontend {
11             Packet packet = frontend.recv();
12             String workerID = "";
13             if packet is TCP {
14                 if new_connection
15                     workerID = availableWorkers.removeFirst();
16                 else
17                     workerID = tcb.getWorkerForPacket(packet);
18             } else
19                 workerID = availableWorkers.removeFirst();
20         }
21
22         Worker worker = getWorker(workerID);
23         worker.send(packet);
24     }
25 }
```

Listing 5.4: Broker's algorithm to decide which worker the data will be sent to

In Listing 5.4, the backend can be simplified to being all the active workers and the frontend the JHCs.

Chapter 6

Implementation

6.1 Overview

Our system is an evolution over our initial proposal [1] and it is written in Java for added performance and portability. The libraries used are either written in native Java or are C/C++ library bindings. Java was chosen because it is a very commonly used language, with a lot of available libraries and community support and it is usually much faster than Python.

There are five core components in our solution: the JHC, the JMS, Clusters, Workers and the Broker, the last three being part of the JDS. So as to maintain the nomenclature used in Briareos, the Clusters, Workers and Broker will henceforth also be named ZClusters, ZWorkers and ZBroker, respectively. Figure 6.1 shows a simplified version of the class diagram of JBriareos. There are changes in relation to Briareos' class diagram [1], but all of them were done in order to simplify and improve the existing system.

6.1.1 Initialization instructions and procedures

To use the JMS, users must first generate ZMQ certificates for both the JMS and any component that is going to be run. The JMS's certificate must then be copied to the other components, and vice-versa. The generation of ZMQ certificates is done by running the `GenerateZMQCertificate` .jar file, like in Listing 6.1:

```
1 # Options: client | cluster | server
2 $ java -jar GenerateZMQCertificate.jar [option]
```

Listing 6.1: Generation of ZMQ certificates

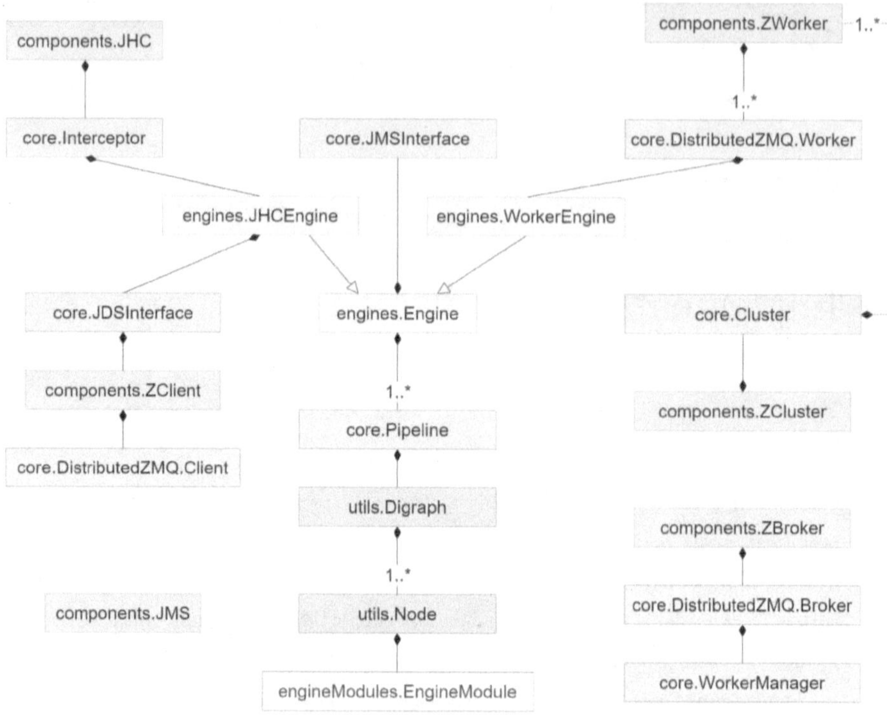

Figure 6.1: JBriareos' simplified class diagram

Before initializing any JHC, users must install NEMO's nfqueue bindings by running the make_lib script, as shown in Listing 6.2.

```
1 $ cd nfQueueBind
2 $ ./make_lib
```

Listing 6.2: Installing the nfqueue bindings

In order to make full use of the system, the JMS should be initialized first, although it does not need to, if the pipeline information was correctly configured in the JHC / ZWorker configuration files. If the JMS is not functional before the initialization of JHCs or ZWorkers, newly created rules will neither be sent nor received and rules that might exist in the JMS will have to be manually created in the host. The ZBroker and ZClusters also do not need to be initialized, but without them it is only possible to perform "inline" packet analysis. Also, in order to be able to utilize them, the user needs to install Docker.

Instructions on how to install Docker are available on

In order to initialize the JMS, execute the respective .jar file, from the root folder of
the project, as shown in Listing 6.3.

```
1 $ java -jar JMS.jar
```

Listing 6.3: Running the JMS

Found existing certificate. Reusing it...
Server PubKey: YfnqBsv6/}.rpeWjvYna@K*6E]l<6Tx@09!&Q<*e
Binding register socket
Binding sink
Binding publisher
Binding responder
Received PING
Received CHECK KEY request
f5715a68-59d8-4b69-8ad9-f9139f6b5180 certificate found...
Distributing rules to a client...
Providing these pipelines:
    ["new_simple_web_app_firewall","new_honeypot_pipeline"]
Received PING
Received CHECK KEY request
32559f40-7913-4d5d-aa5c-dd690467cf9e certificate found...
Received PING
Received CHECK KEY request
32559f40-7913-4d5d-aa5c-dd690467cf9e certificate found...
Providing these pipelines:
    ["new_simple_web_app_firewall"]
Received PING
Received CHECK KEY request
No f3389136-2a17-4859-8311-d25bf731c0c4 certificate found...
Connection from
known JHC
Connection from a
known ZCluster and
a single ZWorker
Connection from
unknown source

Figure 6.2: JMS running

For the sake of parsimony, Figure 6.2 does not contain information about authentication
logs, although these are produced. These logs allow checking connection sources, which is
useful, in example, to map created iptables rules to JHCs or ZClusters.

To initialize the other components, simply follow the same step from when initializing
the JMS, replacing the .jar name with the component to run, like in Listing 6.4.

```
1 # Start a JHC instance
2 $ java -jar JHC.jar
3
4 # Start a ZBroker instance
5 $ java -jar ZBroker.jar
6
7 # Start a ZCluster instance
8 $ java -jar ZCluster.jar
```

Listing 6.4: Running JBriareos' components

Figures 6.3, 6.4, 6.5, and 6.6 showcase the initialization of these components.

```
Found existing certificate...

My CertID: c9790746-8c76-4bd8-ab51-68b44832220c

Checking if the certificate is present on the JMS...
ERROR: Not found
The c9790746-8c76-4bd8-ab51-68b44832220c certificate wasn't found on the JMS...
Couldn't connect to the JMS...
Trying to continue using the local configurations...
Starting JDSInterface
Connecting to ZBroker: tcp://10.132.0.17:10001
JDSInterface is ready
Loading pipelines...
    Loading pipeline 'new_simple_web_app_firewall'
    Loading pipeline 'new_honeypot_pipeline'
2 pipelines loaded

Starting Interceptor
Configuring iptables
Binding queues...
Queues bound: 2
Interceptor is running
JHC is running
```

Figure 6.3: JHC initializing without JMS connection

```
Found existing certificate...

My CertID: f5715a68-59d8-4b69-8ad9-f9139f6b5180

Checking if the certificate is present on the JMS...
Connecting to the JMS on tcp://10.132.0.15:22223
Requesting rules saved on JMS...
Starting JDSInterface
Connecting to ZBroker: tcp://10.132.0.17:10001
JDSInterface is ready
Loading pipelines...
    Loading pipeline 'new simple web app firewall'
    Loading pipeline 'honeypot pipeline'
2 pipelines loaded

Starting Interceptor
Configuring iptables
Binding queues...
Queues bound: 2
Interceptor is running
JHC is running
```

Figure 6.4: JHC initializing with JMS connection

```
Worker Manager address: 'tcp://*:10003' | 'tcp://*:10004'
Starting ZBroker
Frontend address: tcp://*:10001
Backend address: tcp://*:10002
Tasks: 0 | Workers: 0
```

Figure 6.5: ZBroker initializing

```
Initializing Briareos ZCluster
Found existing certificate. Reusing it...
Building ZWorker docker image...
Starting new ZWorker instance
1 containers are running
Connecting to WorkerManager: 'tcp://10.132.0.8:10003' | 'tcp://10.132.0.8:10004'
ZCluster ID: 1592f97d-22dd-45cd-a1a7-701548ebdb36
```

Figure 6.6: ZCluster initializing with JMS connection

6.2 Host Component

In a JHC's initialization phase, its configurations are loaded, an existing ZMQ certificate is read, and the processing engine is initialized, alongside the network interceptor and the JDS and JMS interfaces.

The JMS interface is only initialized if a connection to the JMS can be established, which requires that the JHC has a ZMQ certificate and that it is accepted by the JMS. This is checked via a PING request and a request to verify if the certificate is accepted. If the PING is successful and the certificate accepted, secure communications may be used. On the other hand, if there is no ZMQ certificate, the PING fails, or the certificate is not accepted, the JHC tries to initialize by loading the local configurations. Also, the JMS' public certificate must be present on the JHC, so that the instance has access to the server's public key.

A JHC also has a `start()` and a `stop()` methods. The `start()` method is responsible for starting the network interceptor and, if connected to the JMS, a ZMQ subscriber socket that receives new rules posted by the JBriareos network. The interceptor itself starts the processing engine, which in turn starts both the previously mentioned interfaces. The JMS interface is only started if a connection to the JMS was able to be established. The `stop()` method performs cleanup tasks such as stopping running components and closing sockets before ending the execution.

A JHC configuration file must have information about which pipelines to use. Information about the JMS' address and the ZBroker's has to be present as well, if planing to make use of the information sharing network and distributed processing mode, respectively. Although pipeline configuration in the JHC can be as extensive as the user wants it to be, within the scope provided by JBriareos, if a JHC later requests pipeline information from the JMS, then the JMS' information, if duplicated, will take priority over the one present in the JHC. Listing 6.5 shows an example of a JHC configuration file. The `pipeline` property of this configuration is further explained in section 6.2.1.

```
1  {
2    "pipelines": [
3      {
4        "name": "new_honeypot_pipeline",
5        "port": 7777,
6        "type": "input",
```

```
 7        "verdict": "accept"
 8      },
 9      {
10        "name": "new_simple_web_app_firewall",
11        "port": 4000,
12      },
13    ],
14    "jms": {
15      "ip": "127.0.0.1",
16      "unsecure_port": 11335,
17      "port": 11336,
18      "sink_port": 11337,
19      "publisher_port": 11338
20    },
21    "broker": {
22      "ip": "127.0.0.1",
23      "port": 10001
24    }
25 }
```

Listing 6.5: JHC configuration file example

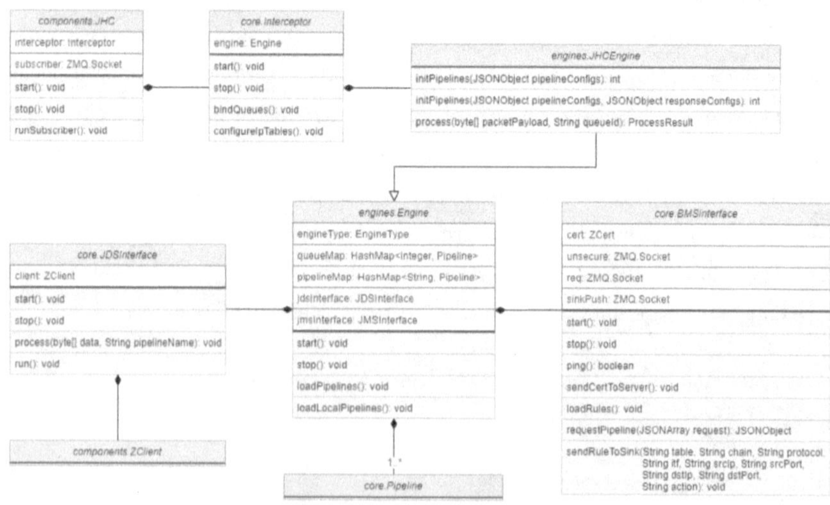

Figure 6.7: JHC's class diagram

6.2.1 Processing Engine

As in Briareos, there are two types of processing engines: a JHC engine and a Worker engine. Both these types extend the Engine class, but differ in functions such as pipeline loading and packet processing. The JHC engine's process function takes into account the processing mode set for a pipeline, while the Worker engine's doesn't, as it only has one single mode of operation. Also, a JHC engine needs to map pipelines to nfqueues but that is not necessary to do in a Worker engine.

During the engine's start, if connected to the JMS, rules present on the server are requested and created locally, pipeline information is requested and the processing pipelines are initialized. If no connection was established, the engine uses the pipeline information present in the JHC configuration file to initialize the pipelines. The JHC engine also initializes both the JDS and JMS interfaces, the latter of which is only started if a connection to the JMS was able to be established, as mentioned previously.

A pipeline configuration file can have the information listed in section 5.2.1.2, in the following fashion:

```
1  {
2      "name": "pipeline_example",
3      "port": 7777,
4      "type": "input",
5      "protocol": "TCP",
6      "interface": "any",
7      "mode": "inline",
8      "verdict": "accept",
9      "modules": [
10         {
11             "name": "Module A",
12             "next": ["Module B", "Module C", "Module D"]
13         },
14         {
15             "name: "Module B",
16             "next": "Module E"
17         },
18         {
19             "name": "Module C",
20             "next": ["Module E", "Module F"]
```

```
21          },
22          {
23              "name": "Module D",
24              "next": "Module F"
25          }
26      ]
27 }
```

Listing 6.6: Pipeline configuration example

Note that the `modules` property is where the pipeline's directed graph is configured. The `name` property references a module, and the `next` property establishes this module's neighbours. With this configuration, a graph like the one shown in Figure 5.3 will be created. All these configurations should be provided in the JHC's or the JMS' configuration files or a mixture of both. If, for example, the JMS' configuration file does not specify a port for a certain pipeline, then that configuration should be present in the JHC's.

The creation of the pipeline graph is done by a `Loader` class, which reads and parses the pipeline configuration. The modules are connected as per the configuration file, making use of custom-made Digraph and Node classes, as shown in Listing 6.7. In this Listing, we create `EngineModules` based on `Strings` referencing them (lines 5-6), checking if their output/input match, and ending the execution if it does not (lines 8-10). We only check that for single input modules, as multiple input modules may receive input with varied types. We then fetch the `UUID` of the node associated with each created module, by checking if their module types match (lines 14-19). If we manage to get `UUIDs` of both the source and the destination nodes, we add a connection between them (lines 21-22, 29-30), otherwise the execution is finished.

```
1 public boolean connectModules(String srcModString,
2                               String dstModString) {
3       UUID srcNodeId = null;
4       UUID dstNodeId = null;
5       EngineModule srcMod =
      EngineModule.createModule(srcModString);
6       EngineModule dstMod =
      EngineModule.createModule(dstModString);
7
8       if (dstMod.getInputMode() == Common.InputMode.SingleInput) {
```

```
 9                if (srcMod.getOutputType() != dstMod.getInputType()) {
10                    return false;
11                }
12            }
13
14        for (Node node : this.graph.getNodes()) {
15            if (node.getModType().equals(srcMod.getModType()))
16                srcNodeId = node.nodeId;
17            else if (node.getModType().equals(dstMod.getModType()))
18                dstNodeId = node.nodeId;
19        }
20
21        if (srcNodeId != null && dstNodeId != null)
22            this.addConnection(srcNodeId, dstNodeId);
23        else
24            return false;
25
26        return true;
27    }
28
29    private void addConnection(UUID srcNodeId, UUID dstNodeId) {
30        this.graph.addConnection(srcNodeId, dstNodeId);
31    }
```

Listing 6.7: Module/Node connection creation functions

The user must make sure that the graph is acyclic, as the Loader class does not verify it. With the configurations shown in Listing 6.8, in which we connect a module with itself, the resulting graph configuration could be accepted, but its outcome would be a never ending packet analysis:

```
1 "modules": [
2     {
3         "name": "Module A",
4         "next": "Module A",
5     }
6 ]
```

Listing 6.8: Erroneous graph configuration example

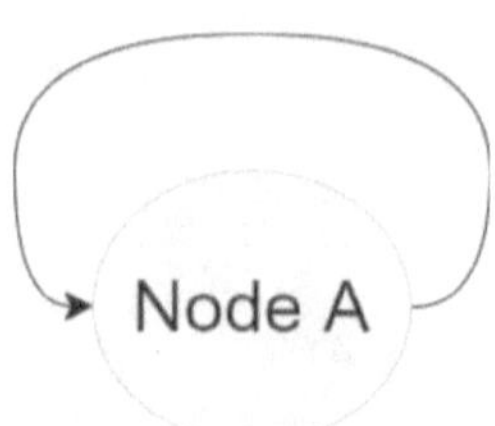

Figure 6.8: Cyclic pipeline graph, provenient of the configuration shown in Listing 6.8

Pipelines also possess a `process()` method, a simplified version of which was shown at Listing 5.1.

6.2.2   Network Interceptor

JBriareos' network interceptor very much follows in the footsteps of his Briareos equivalent. It relies on the netfilterqueue library to perform network traffic interception and packet dissection and modification. It starts by initializing the processing engine so that it in turn loads the pipelines. The loaded pipeline information is then used by the interceptor to create iptables rules using nfqueues. Listing 6.9 shows an example of a pipeline configuration file. Each property of the JSON displayed in the Listing corresponds to an attribute of the pipeline. The definition of these attributes is in section 5.2.1.2.

```
1  {
2      "name": "pipeline_example",
3      "port": 7777,
4      "type": "input",
5      "protocol": "tcp",
6      "interface": "any",
7      "mode": "inline",
8      "verdict": "accept",
9      "modules": [
10         {
11             "name": "Module A",
12         }
13     ]
14 }
```

Listing 6.9: Another pipeline configuration example

```
1 $ iptables -I INPUT -p tcp --dport 7777 -j NFQUEUE --queue-num 1 --queue-
      bypass
```

Listing 6.10: Iptables rule matching the previous pipeline configuration

With the configurations present in Listing 6.9, which are used to create the iptables rule shown in Listing 6.10, incoming TCP packets which are inbound for the port 7777 will be captured and processed by the nfqueue number 1, which is being monitored by the pipeline from which this rule was derived. In this case, the "interface" value is ignored as every interface is subject to that rule by default. The –queue-bypass option is necessary to prevent the default dropping of packets if there is no user-space software listening to the nfqueue in question.

Listing 6.11 shows the method used by the Interceptor to configure iptables rules, based on pipeline configurations. This method were adapted from Briareos. In this Listing, we first get the current nfqueue number (line 3). If that number is -1, then the maximum number of queues has been reached, and the execution is ended (lines 5-8). After getting the current nfqueue number, we check if either the rule will be created on the INPUT chain or the OUTPUT chain of the iptables, as per the pipeline configuration (lines 10-13). We then try to create a nfqueue rule matching the pipeline's attributes, which are defined by its configuration file (line 15), mapping the queue number to the pipeline in question if the creation is successful (line 16), otherwise logging an error (lines 17-18). This process is repeated for each pipeline loaded by the engine (line 2).

```
1  private void configureIpTables() {
2      for (Pipeline pipeline : this.engine.pipelineList) {
3          int queueId = this.getCurrentQueueId();
4
5          if (queueId == -1) {
6              System.out.println("Maximum number of queues reached");
7              return;
8          }
9
10         String chain = IpTables.INPUT_CHAIN;
11         if (pipeline.pipelineType
12                 .equals(Common.PipelineType.OutputPipeline))
13             chain = IpTables.OUTPUT_CHAIN;
```

```
14
15          if (IpTables.createNFQueueRule(queueId, chain,
     pipeline.port, pipeline.protocol, pipeline.itf, pipeline.srcIp))
16              this.engine.queueMap.put(queueId, pipeline);
17          else
18              // Print error
19      }
20  }
```

Listing 6.11: Iptables nfqueues creation

After creating the nfqueues, the interceptor binds them to the matching pipeline, as shown in Listing 6.12.

```
1  private void bindQueues() {
2      for (int queueId : this.engine.queueMap.keySet()) {
3          NetfilterQueue nfQueue =
4                  new NetfilterQueue(queueId, (buf, len) -> {
5
6              Engine.ProcessResult result =
7                  engine.process(buf, String.valueOf(queueId));
8              BPacket bPacket = result.packet;
9              Common.Verdict verdict = result.verdict;
10
11              if (bPacket != null) {
12                  if (bPacket.verdict.equals(Common.Verdict.Accept)) {
13                      if (bPacket.newPayload) {
14                          Ip4Packet packet =
15                              Ip4Packet.parseIp4Packet(buf);
16                          packet.setPayload(bPacket.payload);
17                          return packet.getPacketLength();
18                      }
19
20                      return len;
21                  }
22
23                  return 0;
24              }
```

```
25
26                    if (verdict.equals(Common.Verdict.Accept))
27                        return len;
28
29                    return 0;
30            });
31
32            new Thread(nfQueue::start).start();
33
34            this.nfQueues.addLast(nfQueue);
35        }
36
37        System.out.println("Queues bound: " + this.nfQueues.size());
38 }
```

Listing 6.12: Iptables queue bindings

The handlers shown in Listing 6.12 (lines 3-4) are from nfqueue library bindings withdrawn from the NEMO project. Although in this case the only packets being analysed are IPv4 packets (lines 14-15), it is also possible to analyse packets with other protocols by simply trying to parse them through trial and error. The created handlers call the `process()` method of the processing engine to get a verdict on the captured packet (lines 6-7). Returning 0 (lines 23, 29) is the same as issuing a "DROP" verdict on a packet and returning the packet's length (lines 12-21, 26-27) the same as an "ACCEPT" verdict. In a `ProcessResult`, the packet and the verdict are mutually exclusive, meaning that if one is present in the class, then the other is not, depending on the configured processing mode. If the processing mode is set "inline", then the packet's verdict will be provided in the `BPacket` class, which encompasses the packet itself, otherwise the packet's verdict will always be the default pipeline packet verdict and be provided by itself. These handlers are created for each mapped nfqueue (line 2), in the form of threads (line 32). Finally, the handlers are added to a list (line 34), in order for us to be able to stop them when finishing the execution.

6.2.2.1 BPackets

`BPackets`, which as mentioned were adapted from Briareos and extended to offer more features, are constructed with the captured packet in `byte[]` form and the default verdict of the pipeline through which it is being run through. This class provides utility methods such as parsing the `byte[]` to a NEMO `DataPacket` or getting the captured packet's protocol, source or destination address and port, setting a verdict on the packet, and so forth, as shown in Figure 6.9.

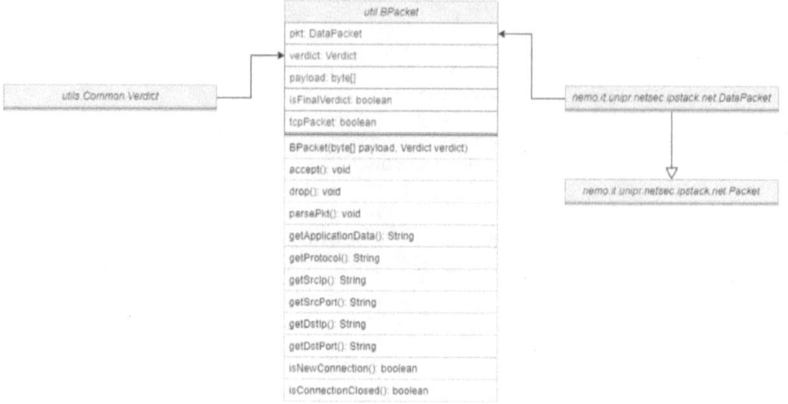

Figure 6.9: BPacket's class diagram

Other utility methods can easily be added if and when needed. As this version of JBriareos only accepts IPv4 TCP and UDP packets, a simple boolean variable is enough to check the type of the packet, although adding support for other protocols is very doable, as the NEMO library provides an extensive list of protocols such as ARP, Ethernet and OSPF, in which case that boolean could become, in example, an enumeration.

6.2.3   Modules

Modules are classes that extend the `EngineModule` class. Although the use of modules was imported from Briareos, we overhauled most of their features in order to provide a more structured, rigid and failure-proof way of implementing new modules. Every module must have an exclusive `ModuleType` (Listing 6.13), which is used to identify the module when creating a node in the pipeline's graph. When creating a new module, a `ModuleType` must be added in the corresponding enumeration.

```
1  public enum ModuleType {
2      AppDataFilter ,
3      PidFetcher ,
4      SignatureTest
```

```
5  }
```

Listing 6.13: ModuleType example

It must also be possible to map a **String** to a **ModuleType**, as shown in Listing 6.14, to be used when initializing a module after reading its name from a configuration file.

```
1  public EngineModule(ModuleType modType) {
2      this.modType = modType;
3  }
4
5  public static EngineModule createModule(String modName) {
6      switch (modName) {
7          case "app_data_filter":
8              return new AppDataFilter();
9          case "pid_fetcher":
10             return new PidFetcher();
11         case "signature_test_module":
12             return new SignatureTest();
13         default:
14             System.out.println("There is no module with that name");
15     }
16
17     return null;
18 }
```

Listing 6.14: EngineModule initialization example

As displayed in Listing 6.15, a module must also specify its own input and output type (lines 6-14), input mode (lines 17-19) and implement a process method (lines 22-33). The module shown in this Listing, which was also a Briareos module, returns the PID and application name of the process which is sending/receiving the captured packet. This implementation utilizes a custom-made class similar to a OpenSnitch's class that serves a similar but more complex purpose [49]. OpenSnitch is a linux/GNU version of Little Snitch, a host-based application firewall for MacOS [50].

```
1  public class PidFetcher extends EngineModule {
2      public PidFetcher() {
```

```java
3            super(ModuleType.PidFetcher);
4        }
5
6        @Override
7        public IOType getInputType() {
8            return IOType.None;
9        }
10
11       @Override
12       public IOType getOutputType() {
13           return IOType.Tuple;
14       }
15
16       @Override
17       public Common.InputMode getInputMode() {
18           return Common.InputMode.SingleInput;
19       }
20
21       @Override
22       public ModuleIO process(BPacket packet, ModuleIO data,
       JMSInterface jmsInterface) {
23           String srcIp = packet.getSrcIp();
24           int srcPort = packet.getSrcPort();
25           String dstIp = packet.getDstIP();
26           int dstPort = packet.getDstPort();
27
28           PsUtil.ConnectionAppInfo appInfo =
       PsUtil.getPidFromNetConnections(packet.getProtocol(), srcIp,
       srcPort, dstIp, dstPort);
29           if (appInfo == null)
30               appInfo = new PsUtil.ConnectionAppInfo(-1, "Unknown");
31
32           return new ModuleIO(IOType.Tuple, new
       IOData.IOTuple(appInfo.pid, appInfo.appName));
33       }
34  }
```

Listing 6.15: `PidFetcher` module

In the **process** method of Listing 6.15, initially we fetch the source and destination IP addresses and ports of the captured packet (lines 23-26), using them in conjunction with the packet's protocol to get information about which process is receiving it (line 28). If that information is `null`, then there is no record of that connection (line 30), otherwise we return a `ModuleIO` with type `IOType.Tuple` and the software's PID and name as a `IOData.IOTuple` (line 32).

Every module's process method must return a `ModuleIO`. This is done to ease the passage of output from a module to another module's input. Listing 6.16, complemented by Listings 6.17 and 6.18, showcases the `ModuleIO` class.

```
1  public class ModuleIO {
2      public IOType ioType;
3      public IOData ioData;
4
5      public ModuleIO(IOType ioType, IOData ioData) {
6          this.ioType = ioType;
7          this.ioData = ioData;
8      }
9
10     public ModuleIO() {
11         this.ioType = IOType.None;
12         this.ioData = null;
13     }
14 }
```

Listing 6.16: `ModuleIO` class

```
1  public enum IOType {
2      None,
3      String,
4      List,
5      HTTPObject,
6      Tuple
7  }
```

Listing 6.17: `IOType` enumeration

```java
public class IOData {
    public static class IOString extends IOData {
        public String string;

        public IOString(String string) {
            this.string = string;
        }
    }

    public static class IOList extends IOData {
        public LinkedList<ModuleIO> list;

        public IOList(LinkedList<ModuleIO> list) {
            this.list = list;
        }
    }

    public static class IOHttpObj extends IOData {
        public HttpObject httpObject;

        public IOHttpObj(HttpObject httpObject) {
            this.httpObject = httpObject;
        }
    }

    public static class IOTuple extends IOData {
        public long number;
        public String string;

        public IOTuple(long number, String string) {
            this.number = number;
            this.string = string;
        }
    }
}
```

Listing 6.18: IOData extensible class

Other `IOTypes` can be added and the `IOData` class extended to create new IO types as needed by newly created modules.

6.3 Distributed Offloading System

The JDS implementation is very similar to its Briareos equivalent. It utilizes ZeroMQ sockets to transmit information and Docker containers as workers to process received packets. There are also four main components in this JDS: a ZClient, the ZBroker, ZClusters and ZWorkers. A ZClient is contained in the JHC and sends tasks to the ZBroker, which in turn distributes them using the LRU algorithm described in Listing 5.4.

6.3.1 ZClient

The ZClient is the `JDSInterface` component that establishes a connection from a JHC to the ZBroker. Tasks to be sent from the JHC to the distributed offloading system are put in a queue and afterwards consumed by the ZClient. These tasks contain the captured packet in `byte[]` format and an identification of the pipeline through which the packet should be run. This component was mostly used "as-was" on Briareos, and, just like in it, a client connects to the broker using a DEALER/ROUTER connection type, where the former is the dealer and the latter the router. Listing 6.19 showcases the `JDSInterface`, and Listing 6.20 the ZClient.

In the **process** method of Listing 6.19 (lines 18-20), a `QueueObject` containing the captured packet in `byte[]` form (stored in the `data` variable), and a pipeline's name is inserted into a multiple producer, single consumer queue (line 19). In the **run** method of the same listing, we continuously try to fetch objects from that queue (line 26), sending then to be processed by the client when the operation is successful (lines 27-28).

In the **process** method of Listing 6.20, the information received from the `JDSInterface` is then offloaded to the broker (lines 13-14).

```
1   public class JDSInterface implements Runnable {
2       private static class QueueObject {
3           byte[] data;
4           String pipelineName;
5           QueueObject(byte[] data, String pipelineName) {
6               this.data = data;
7               this.pipelineName = pipelineName;
```

```
8          }
9      }
10
11     ZClient client;
12     MpscLinkedQueue<QueueObject> queue;
13     public JDSInterface() {
14         this.client = new ZClient();
15         this.queue = new MpscLinkedQueue<>();
16     }
17
18     public void process(byte[] data, String pipelineName) {
19         this.queue.offer(new QueueObject(data, pipelineName));
20     }
21
22     @Override
23     public void run() {
24         while (true) {
25             try {
26                 QueueObject obj = this.queue.poll();
27                 if (obj != null)
28                     this.client.process(obj.data, obj.pipelineName);
29             } catch (InterruptedException ignored) { return; }
30         }
31     }
32 }
```

Listing 6.19: JDSInterface

```
1 public ZClient() {
2     this.id = UUID.randomUUID();
3     this.context = new ZContext();
4     this.connection = context.createSocket(SocketType.DEALER);
5     this.connection.setIdentity(id.toString().getBytes());
6 }
7
8 public void start() {
9     this.connection.connect(this.brokerAddress);
```

```
10  }
11
12  public void process(byte[] data, String extraParam) {
13      this.connection.send(data, ZMQ.SNDMORE);
14      this.connection.send(extraParam);
15  }
```

Listing 6.20: A client's constructor and start and process methods

6.3.2 ZBroker

The ZBroker, as in Briareos, can be divided into a Worker Manager and an algorithm that
serves as a broker interface between the frontend, the JHCs, and the backend, the workers.
Communications are handled by two ZMQ ROUTER sockets, one for each of the ends. A
ZBroker configuration file, examplified in Listing 6.21, must specify its sockets' frontend,
backend and Worker Manager's ports, as well as the interval for the Worker Manager to
request usage statistics from the ZClusters.

```
1  {
2    "broker": {
3      "frontend": {
4        "port": 10001
5      },
6      "backend": {
7        "port": 10002
8      },
9      "worker_manager": {
10        "port": 10003,
11        "sink_port": 10004,
12        "interval": 20
13      }
14    }
15  }
```

Listing 6.21: ZBroker configuration file example

The Worker Manager launches three different threads, each executing a different run
method:

- **runPublisher()**: Running this method, a thread is tasked with requesting clusters their workers' usage statistics;

- **runSink()**: Running this method, a thread is tasked with collecting and processing the worker statistics sent by the clusters;

- **run()**: Running this method, a thread is tasked with updating each cluster's and the overall system's usage metrics and, if necessary, sending a notification to a cluster for it to start or stop worker instances.

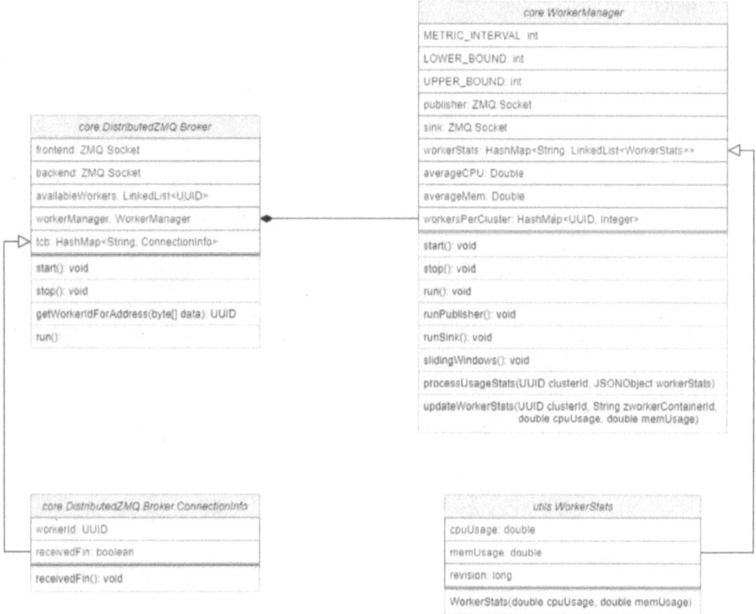

Figure 6.10: ZBroker's class diagram

A simplified example of the Worker Manager's **run()** method can be found in Listing 5.3.

Listing 6.22 showcases the broker's **run** method. The broker constantly polls both the frontend (if there are available workers, lines 23-24) and the backend (line 4). Messages from the frontend (lines 25-27) are brokered to workers (lines 31-35), which are chosen with a custom method that takes into account the connection protocol and existing connections (line 28). Messages from the backend (lines 5-10) are either connections from new workers (lines 11-12) or results of a brokered packet analysis task (lines 13-20). If a result of an analysis was the drop of a packet, that packet is logged (lines 15-18). A simplified version of this algorithm is displayed in Listing 5.4

```java
1  public void run() {
2      while (true) {
3          this.poller.poll();
4          if (this.poller.pollin(0)) {  // Poll the backend
5              UUID workerId = UUID.fromString(
6                      this.backend.recvStr());
7
8              this.availableWorkers.addLast(workerId);
9              this.backend.recvStr(); // Empty
10             String clientMsg = this.backend.recvStr();
11             if (clientMsg.equals(Worker.READY_MSG)) {
12                 System.out.println("New worker: " + workerId);
13             } else {
14                 String result = this.backend.recvStr();
15                 if (result.equals(
16                         String.valueOf(Common.Verdict.Drop))) {
17                     byte[] data = this.backend.recv();
18                     System.out.println(new BPacket(data));
19                 }
20             }
21         }
22
23         if (!this.availableWorkers.isEmpty()) {
24             if (this.poller.pollin(1)) {  // Poll the frontend
25                 String clientId = this.frontend.recvStr();
26                 byte[] data = this.frontend.recv();
27                 String pipelineName = this.frontend.recvStr();
28                 String workerId = getWorkerIdForAddress(data);
29
30                 // Broker the information
31                 this.backend.send(workerId, ZMQ.SNDMORE);
32                 this.backend.send("", ZMQ.SNDMORE);
33                 this.backend.send(clientId, ZMQ.SNDMORE);
34                 this.backend.send(data, ZMQ.SNDMORE);
```

```
35                    this.backend.send(pipelineName);
36            }
37        }
38    }
39 }
```

Listing 6.22: The broker's `run()` method

6.3.3   ZCluster

ZClusters connect to the broker's Worker Manager via push/pull and publisher/subscriber sockets, the configuration of which must be present in its configuration file (Listing 6.23). This file must also have configured the JMS's "unsecure" socket, so that the cluster is able to check if its ZMQ certificate, which will be used by its workers, is accepted by the JMS.

```
1 {
2    "cluster": {
3      "worker_manager": {
4        "ip": "127.0.0.1",
5        "port": 10003,
6        "sink_port": 10004
7      },
8      "jms": {
9        "ip": "127.0.0.1",
10       "unsecure_port": 11335
11     }
12   }
13 }
```

Listing 6.23: ZCluster configuration file example

Clusters build the workers' Docker image on startup, in order to share with them its own and the JMS's ZMQ certificate. In that manner, workers are then able to utilize the cluster's certificate as if it was their own, and establish secure communications with the JMS.

A Cluster's Docker client is used to start or stop ZWorker instances running on Docker containers, as shown in Listing 6.24.

```java
private void buildDockerImage() {
    try {
        ProcessBuilder processBuilder = new ProcessBuilder();
        processBuilder.command("bash", "-c",
                Common.DOCKER_IMAGE_BUILDER);

        Process process = processBuilder.start();
        process.waitFor();
    } catch (Exception ignored) {
        // Print error
    }
}

private void startNewInstance() {
    CreateContainerResponse response = this.dockerClient
            .createContainerCmd(DOCKER_IMAGE_NAME)
            .withHostConfig(new HostConfig()
                    .withNetworkMode("host")
                    .withCpuQuota(CPU_QUOTA))
            .exec();

    this.dockerClient.startContainerCmd(response.getId()).exec();
    this.numInstances++;
}

private void stopInstance() {
    List<Container> containerList =
        this.dockerClient.listContainersCmd().exec();
    if (!containerList.isEmpty()) {
        String containerId = containerList.get(0).getId();
        this.dockerClient.stopContainerCmd(containerId).exec();
        this.dockerClient.removeContainerCmd(containerId).exec();
    }
}

private void stopAllInstances() {
    for (Container container :
```

```
38          this.dockerClient.listContainersCmd().exec()) {

39
        this.dockerClient.stopContainerCmd(container.getId()).exec();

40
        this.dockerClient.removeContainerCmd(container.getId()).exec();

41      }

42  }
```

Listing 6.24: A cluster's methods that use Docker

Listing 6.25 showcases the ZClusters' **run** method, which was adapted from Briareos. This method waits to receive information from the Worker Manager (line 4), and executes a series of instructions depending on the task received (lines 6-18).

```
1  public void run() {
2      while (true) {
3          try {
4              String data = this.publisher.recvStr();
5              switch (data) {
6                  case WorkerManager.USAGE_MSG:
7                      JSONObject usageStats = this.getUsageStats();
8                      this.sink.send(this.clusterId.toString());
9                      this.sink.send(usageStats.toJSONString());
10                     break;
11                 case WorkerManager.START_NEW_INSTANCE_MSG:
12                     String clusterId = data.split(" ")[2];
13                     if (this.clusterId.toString().equals(clusterId))
14                         this.startNewInstance();
15                     break;
16                 case WorkerManager.STOP_INSTANCE_MSG:
17                     this.stopInstance();
18                     break;
19             }
20         } catch (RuntimeException ignored) {
21             return;
22         }
23     }
24  }
```

Listing 6.25: A cluster's **run()** method

The **getUsageStats()** method, part of which is shown in Listing 6.26, makes use of the Docker client to fetch the CPU and memory usage metrics of each container managed by the cluster.

```
1  // (...)
2  InvocationBuilder.AsyncResultCallback<Statistics> callback =
3      new InvocationBuilder.AsyncResultCallback<>();
4  this.dockerClient.statsCmd(container.getId()).exec(callback);
5  Statistics stats = callback.awaitResult();
6  callback.close();
7  double cpuUsage = this.getCpuUsage(stats);
8  double memUsage = this.getMemUsage(stats);
9  // (...)
```

Listing 6.26: Part of the **getUsageStats()** method

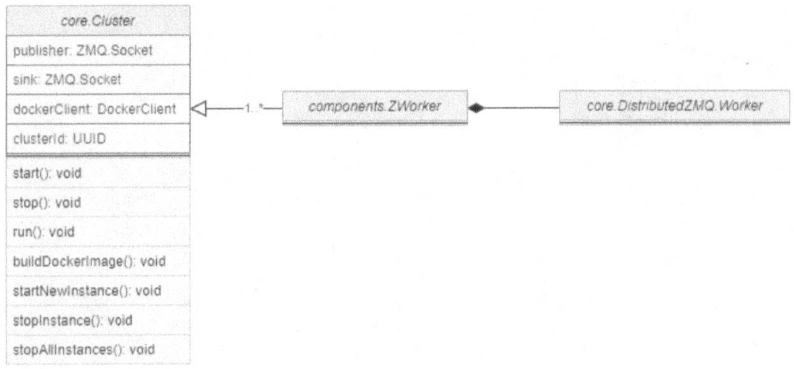

Figure 6.11: ZCluster's class diagram

6.3.4 ZWorker

A ZWorker is the distributed offloading system's component that performs computation on a packet captured by a JHC and send to the JDS. Its engine differs from a JHC's in that there is simply one processing mode, inline, it does not need to worry about ports

when loading pipelines and it does not possess a JDS interface, as it is part of the JDS
itself. Just like a JHC, a worker does not need to be connected to the JMS to function,
but if it does not then it cannot share newly created rules.

A worker's configuration file (Listing 6.27) must specify the broker's, worker manager's
and JMS' every address and ports, as well as the processing pipelines to load.

```
 1 {
 2   "worker": {
 3     "broker": {
 4       "ip": "127.0.0.1",
 5       "port": 10002
 6     },
 7     "worker_manager": {
 8       "ip": "127.0.01",
 9       "port": 10003,
10       "sink_port": 10004
11     },
12     "jms": {
13       "ip": "127.0.0.1",
14       "unsecure_port": 11335,
15       "port": 11336,
16       "sink_port": 11337,
17       "publisher_port": 11338
18     },
19     "pipelines": [
20       {
21         "name": "new_simple_web_app_firewall",
22       }
23     ]
24   }
25 }
```

Listing 6.27: ZWorker configuration file example

A worker initially connects to the broker and sends a message that notifies the latter
of the former's existence. After that, it waits for a task to be received, sending it to be
processed by its engine when it is and replying to the broker after it is completed. The
reply is the verdict issued on the packet. If the verdict was to drop it, then the packet

will be sent as well, so that it may be manually inspected. Listing 6.28 showcases the
ZWorkers' **run** method. This method waits to receive a task from the broker (lines 5-7),
processes it (lines 8-9) and sends the result back to the broker (lines 10-19). If the resulting
verdict was to drop the packet, then the packet itself is sent back to the broker, alongside
the verdict (lines 11-15), otherwise only the latter is sent (lines 18-19).

```
1  public void run() {
2      this.connection.send(Worker.READY_MSG);
3      while (true) {
4          try {
5              String address = this.connection.recvStr();
6              byte[] data = this.connection.recv();
7              String extraParam = this.connection.recvStr();
8              Engine.ProcessResult result =
9                  this.engine.process(data, extraParam);
10             this.connection.send(address, ZMQ.SNDMORE);
11             if (result.packet.verdict == Common.Verdict.Drop) {
12                 this.connection.send(
13                     String.valueOf(result.packet.verdict),
14                     ZMQ.SNDMORE);
15                 this.connection.send(data);
16             }
17             else
18                 this.connection.send(
19                     String.valueOf(result.packet.verdict));
20         } catch (RuntimeException ignored) {
21             return;
22         }
23     }
24 }
```

Listing 6.28: A worker's run() method

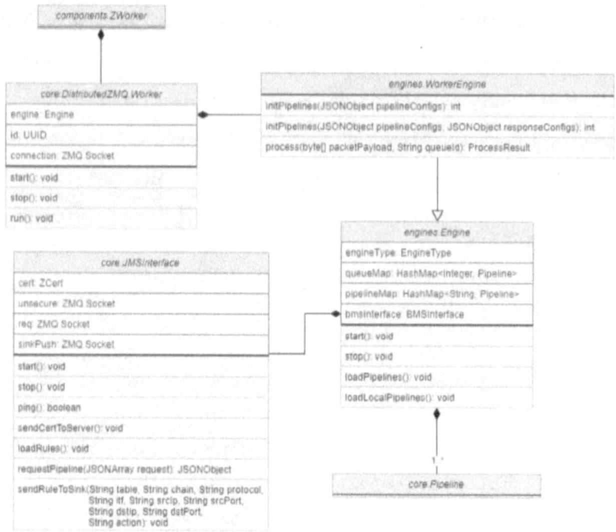

Figure 6.12: ZWorker's class diagram

6.4 Manager Server

The JMS is the JBriareos' component responsible for handling iptables rules and pipeline configurations deployment. Its configuration file must specify its ports, like so:

```
1 {
2   "jms": {
3     "unsecure_port": 11335,
4     "port": 11336,
5     "sink_port": 11337,
6     "publisher_port": 11338
7   }
8 }
```

Listing 6.29: JMS' configuration file

These four ports, indicate, by writing order, the port which handles unsecure communications, such as pings or verifying if some certificate is accepted; the port that handles simple request-reply communications, used for rules and pipelines deployment; the port which receives newly created rules from other components; and the port which publishes them.

If some rule is to be created in new instances at startup, then it should be written in a specific file in the JMS so that it may be deployed during the initial JHC-JMS connection.

```
1  [
2      {
3          "chain": "INPUT",
4          "protocol": "udp",
5          "action": "DROP"
6      },
7      {
8          "table"; "nat",
9          "chain": "PREROUTING",
10         "action": "DNAT --to-destination 10.0.2.15"
11         "srcIp": "189.233.10.128"
12     }
13 ]
```

Listing 6.30: Rules' file example

Listing 6.30 examplifies how iptables rules are stored on the JMS. The first rule drops every incoming UDP packet. The second rule redirects to 10.0.2.15, packets from 189.233.10.128. These rules are equivalent to running the following commands:

```
1 # The first rule
2 iptables -I INPUT -p udp -j DROP
3
4 # The second rule
5 iptables -t nat -I PREROUTING -s 189.233.10.128 -j DNAT --to-destination
      10.0.2.15
```

Listing 6.31: Iptables rules matching those written in Listing 6.30

If some attack is discovered and a rule is created and sent to the JMS, then, before it is propagated through the network, it will be written in this file, so that it may be applied to JHC instances entering the JBriareos network afterwards.

Pipeline configurations parameters present in the JMS will be prioritised over those present in JHCs or Workers, as mentioned previously in section 6.2.

If a connection to the JMS is able to be established by a JHC or Worker then their engines will initialize a JMS interface class, which handles every communication with the JMS.

The JMS is not dependent upon any other part of JBriareos to run.

<table>
<tr><td>

components.JMS

auth: ZAuth
cert: ZCert
unsecure: ZMQ.Socket
rep: ZMQ.Socket
publisher: ZMQ.Socket
sink: ZMQ.Socket
start(): void
stop(): void
ping(): boolean
runUnsecure(): void
run(): void
runSink(): void

</td><td>

core.JMSInterface

cert: ZCert
unsecure: ZMQ.Socket
req: ZMQ.Socket
sinkPush: ZMQ.Socket
start(): void
stop(): void
ping(): boolean
sendCertToServer(): void
loadRules(): void
requestPipeline(JSONArray request): JSONObject
sendRuleToSink(String table, String chain, String protocol, String itf, String srcIp, String srcPort, String dstIp, String dstPort, String action): void

</td></tr>
</table>

Figure 6.13: JMS' (on the left) and its interface's (on the right) class diagrams

Listing 6.32 showcases the JMS's **run** methods. Each method is executed in a different thread.

The **run** method (lines 1-13), waits for messages (line 4), sending the stored iptables rules (line 6) or pipeline configurations (line 8), depending on the received message.

The **runUnsecure** method (lines 15-29), is similar to the previous **run** method, in that it waits for messages (line 18), and replies to requests (lines 19-24).

The **runSink** method (lines 31-64) receives a **String** from a ZMQ socket (line 36), parses it into a JSON object (line 37), and tries to form a iptables rule from it (lines 39-43). After checking that a rule can be formed, the JMS schedules a task to write that rule to the rules file (lines 45-56). The scheduler is executed immediately (line 56), but if the file is locked, it is rescheduled (lines 50-53). In the end, the JMS publishes the newly created rule to all the host components (line 58).

```
1   private void run() {
2       while (true) {
3           try {
4               String request = this.rep.recvStr();
5               if (request.equals("GET RULES"))
6                   sendRules();
7               else
```

```java
 8                  sendPipelines(request);
 9              } catch (RuntimeException ignored) {
10                  return;
11              }
12          }
13  }
14
15  private void runUnsecure() {
16      while (true) {
17          try {
18              String request = this.unsecure.recvStr();
19              if (request.equals("CHECK KEY")) {
20                  checkKey();
21              } else if (request.equals("PING")) {
22                  this.unsecure.send("OK");
23              } else
24                  this.unsecure.send("Unknown request: " + request);
25          } catch (RuntimeException ignored) {
26              return;
27          }
28      }
29  }
30
31  private void runSink() {
32      JSONParser parser = new JSONParser();
33
34      while (true) {
35          try {
36              String jsonString = this.sink.recvStr();
37              JSONObject ruleOptions = (JSONObject)
      parser.parse(jsonString);
38
39              try {
40                  IpTables.formRuleFromJSON(ruleOptions);
41              } catch (Exception ignored) {
42                  continue;
43              }
44
```

```java
45              Runnable writeRuleToFileRunnable = new Runnable() {
46                  @Override
47                  public void run() {
48                      try {
49                          writeRuleToFile(ruleOptions);
50                      } catch (IOException ignored) {
51                          // The file is locked, as it is being read
52                          scheduler.schedule(this, 2,
    TimeUnit.SECONDS);
53                      }
54                  }
55              };
56              scheduler.schedule(writeRuleToFileRunnable, 0,
    TimeUnit.SECONDS);
57
58              this.publisher.send(jsonString);
59          } catch (RuntimeException ignored) {
60              return;
61          } catch (ParseException ignored) {
62          }
63      }
64 }
```

Listing 6.32: JMS' run methods

Chapter 7

Results

With Briareos as our starting point, we managed to implement JBriareos, a scalable HIDPS solution that offers a good overall performance. We offer a simple, easy and structured way to expand the modular framework and we have ported each and every single Briareos module to JBriareos. Some cleanup problems stemming for closing ZMQ sockets and contexts were fixed and the system is overall more stable, as it implements more failure-checking conditions. The ZBroker now also collects workers' packet analysis results and is able to show them, and takes into consideration a packet's transport protocol before attributing that task to a worker.

By implementing the JMS, we were able to protect the entire system from attacks that a single instance has detected. If a packet is sent to the JDS and an attack is detected by a worker, the whole system can be retroactively protected, if a rule is sent from that Worker to the JMS, which propagates it to the JHC instances. This makes it so that, in JBriareos, the JDS is able to also protect JHC instances from attacks, instead of simply detecting that attacks occurred, which is not the case for Briareos' JDS. Pipeline configuration files are also now able to be kept centralized and rules created by the system be persistent, as they are stored in the JMS.

A drawback of using JBriareos when compared to Briareos is that every time modules are created, the JHC's and ZWorker's .jar files must be updated, which makes it a bit inconvenient to an administrator, as they must afterwards be redeployed to the machines running them. Using Briareos, only the new module's Python files must be deployed.

We were not able to implement our modules on other systems (such as Zeek), nor implement the main functionalities of other systems on our own (such as Tripwire's or OSSEC's filesystem checks). Under those circumstances, our only option was to compare

JBriareos with its predecessor, Briareos. Furthermore, in the case of comparing our system with Tripwire or OSSEC, we must keep in mind that computations performed by the systems are triggered differently. JBriareos' is triggered when a packet is captured by nfqueues, whereas the others are performed periodically, or when filesystem changes are detected.

7.1   Performance comparison

For comparing the performance of both Briareos and JBriareos host components, a virtual machine with 4 virtual Intel Xeon CPU @2.30GHz cores and 8GB of RAM was used. This host was running a small, simple file sharing Node.js HTTP server and a host component instance. The JMS was also running in a 4vCPUs, 8GB of RAM virtual machine, as well as the JDS's Broker and any clusters used.

The information collected is the average response time of the server, with an assortment of different running pipelines. Only one pipeline was active at a time, and any pipeline used had at least one module and at most three. Computation performed by the modules varied from simply checking a packet's payload for a pattern, building HTTP objects, dissecting and analysing HTTP requests, monitoring the system and its connections, etc. For all graphs except the one in Figure 7.2, the vertical error bars represent the variance of the results. In this last figure, the vertical bars represent the standard deviation of the results, instead of the variance, as the latter is too high.

Analysing the results obtained, it can be seen that although offloading tasks to the distributed offloading system is basically the same in both versions (Figure 7.3), which is expected, as basically no computation is actually done by the host, JBriareos' engines process captured packets much faster than their Python counterparts (Figures 7.1 and 7.2). Although the server's response times seem to grow linearly with both systems, that growth is much slower in JBriareos' case. In fact, JBriareos is, on average, 85.28% ($\pm$ 1.5%) faster than Briareos, considering every case tested. In other words, Briareos is more than five times slower than JBriareos, when it comes to packet analysis.

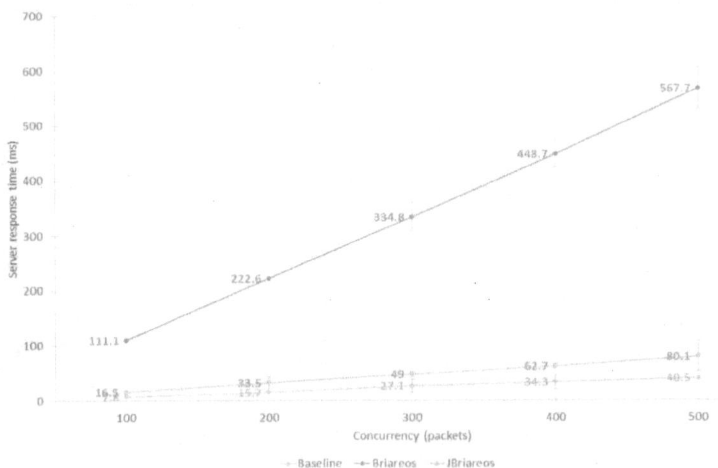

Figure 7.1: Performance comparison for inline processing

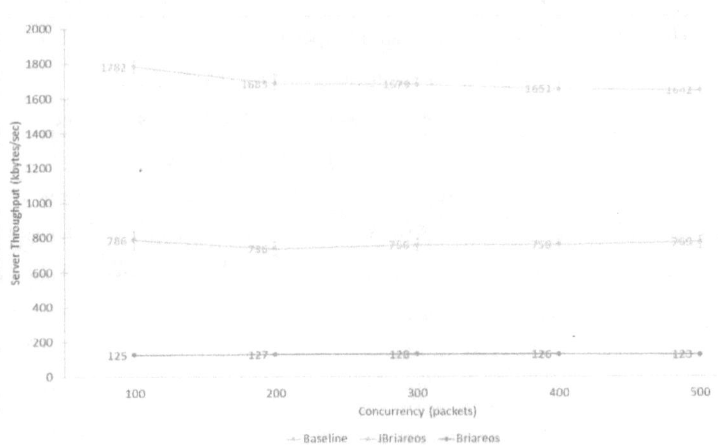

Figure 7.2: Throughput comparison for inline processing

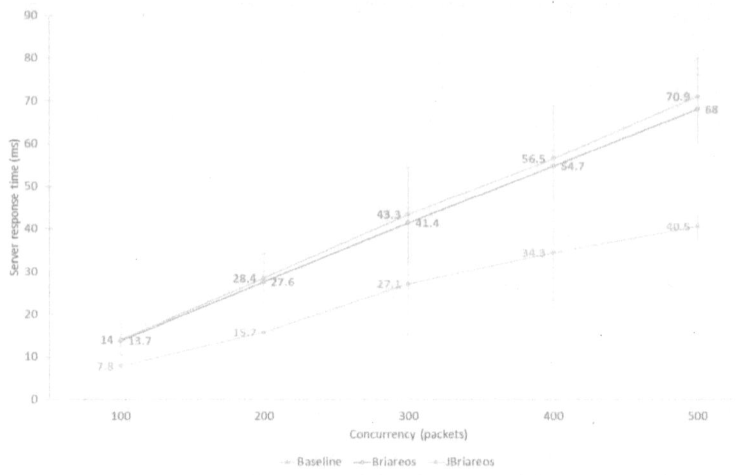

Figure 7.3: Performance comparison for offloading tasks to the JDS

7.1.1 JDS performance

For our next tests, we set the JHC to offload tasks to the JDS. We wanted to measure how much time it would take the JDS to compute 500k tasks, offloaded from a JHC instance. These tasks are the same we used when analysing the performance of the JHCs, except they were offloaded to the JDS, which was set up to use 1, 2 or 4 clusters, depending on the test. Each cluster was initialized by default with 1 worker instance, but could start more if their workers' average CPU or memory usage was over 60%.

As was expected, the JDS is able to process tasks faster, the more clusters/workers are used (Figure 7.4) and the more workers used, the less average CPU usage of each individual worker (Figure 7.5). As for the memory usage (Figure 7.6), we can observe that it maintains constant, regardless of the number of clusters/workers used. This can be explained by the fact that the executed processing modules used a static amount of memory (only dependent on the size of the packet to analyse), which results in the same memory amount being used by every worker.

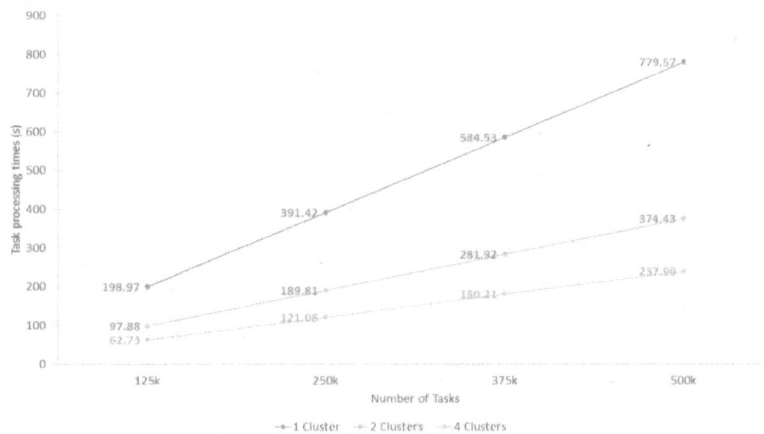

Figure 7.4: Performance measurements of the JDS, with different numbers of clusters

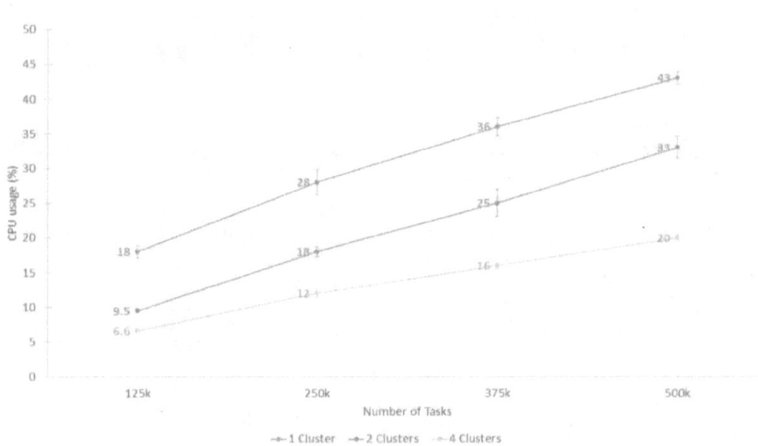

Figure 7.5: Average CPU usage per worker, with different numbers of clusters

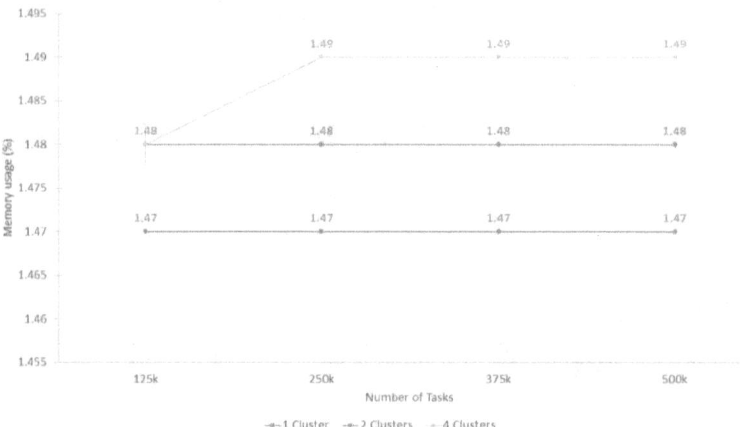

Figure 7.6: Average memory usage per worker, with different numbers of clusters

7.2   JMS rule sharing and pipeline configuration distribution

The implementation of the JMS was also very successful. A simulation of an attack was
run, in which the objective was to trigger a module that creates an iptables rule to block
any incoming packet from the attacker's address, if an attack is detected. Listings 7.1, 7.2,
and 7.3 showcase the pipeline configurations present in the JHC, workers and the JMS,
respectively.

```
1 "pipelines": [
2   {
3     "name": "new_simple_web_app_firewall",
4     "port": 4000,
5     "mode": "distributed"
6   }
7 ]
```

Listing 7.1: Pipeline configurations on the JHC

```
1 "pipelines": [
2   {
3     "name": "new_simple_web_app_firewall",
4   }
5 ]
```

Listing 7.2: Pipeline configurations on the ZWorkers

```
1 {
2   "type": "input",
3   "protocol": "TCP",
4   "interface": "any",
5   "verdict": "accept",
6   "modules": [
7     {
8       "name": "app_data_filter"
9     }
10   ]
```

```
11 }
```

Listing 7.3: Pipeline configurations on the JMS

Listing 7.4 showcases the **process** method of the **AppDataFilter** module. It checks a packet's payload for a specific pattern, which is, in this case, the word "hack".

```
 1  public ModuleIO process(BPacket packet, ModuleIO data, JMSInterface
        jmsInterface) {
 2      String packetData = packet.getApplicationData();
 3      if (packetData.isEmpty()) {
 4          packet.accept();
 5          return new ModuleIO();
 6      }
 7
 8      if (packetData.contains("hack")) {
 9          packet.drop();
10
11          if (jmsInterface != null)    // Try to send rule to JMS
12              jmsInterface.blockIPAddress(packet);
13          else                         // Just block it locally
14              packet.blockIPAddress();
15      }
16
17      return new ModuleIO(IOType.String,
18              new IOData.IOString(packetData));
19  }
```

Listing 7.4: AppDataFilter module's process method

The JHC was set to offload captured packets, which means that it was a Worker that detected the attack and propagated the rule.

In Figure 7.7, it is shown the JMS logging that it received an iptables rule to propagate. Although the JMS does not know from where that rule came from, it does not matter, because only JHC and Worker instances that are able to establish secure communications with the JMS are able to send newly created rules to it.

In Figure 7.8, it is shown that the JHC running on the server received a rule from the JMS, and tried to create it locally.

```
Received rule:
    iptables -I INPUT -s 189.34.94.2 -j DROP
Publishing the received rule...
```

Figure 7.7: Reception and propagation of an iptables rule by the JMS

```
JHC is running
Received rule...
    -> iptables -I INPUT -s 189.34.94.2 -j DROP
Creating rule locally...
```

Figure 7.8: Reception and creation of an iptables rule by the JHC

In Figure 7.9, it is shown the INPUT chain of the iptables rules present on the host. There are two iptables rules. The first is the rule that was published by the JMS. The second is the rule that was created by the loading of the processing pipelines. Incidentally, it is possible to know that the IP address 189.34.94.2, which is the IP address chosen in the attack simulation, corresponds to the domain name bd225e02.virtua.com.br. As the packet analysis task was offloaded, the first packet sent from that address was accepted, as per the pipeline's configurations, but further attempts were dropped. If the pipeline was set for inline packet analysis, or had a default verdict to DROP packets, then not even the first packet would be accepted.

```
# iptables -L
Chain INPUT (policy ACCEPT)
target     prot opt source                destination
DROP       all  --  bd225e02.virtua.com.br  anywhere
NFQUEUE    tcp  --  anywhere              anywhere            tcp dpt:4000 NFQUEUE num 0 bypass
```

Figure 7.9: iptables INPUT chain on the JHC host

As can be seen in Figures 6.2 and 6.4, the pipeline configuration distribution feature of the JMS is also working perfectly, and it can be seen in Figure 6.3 that even without the JMS, the system has no problems functioning. The JMS should always the used, as it saves iptables rules created by the components that perform packet analysis, but it does not need to, specially in cases where the network consists of only one JHC instance and no JDS.

Chapter 8

Conclusion

In conclusion, we were able to build a scalable HIDPS with an easily expandable modular framework and good performance, that is capable of both analysing a network's traffic and monitoring the host's system. With the JDS, we are able to offload tasks and spare the hosts' resources and we also implemented information sharing features that provide safety to every host, in the case of an attack being detected by any one of them.

With the addition of the JMS, we were able to centralize pipeline configuration files so that an administrator has a much easier time handling them, and propagate iptables rules created by one component to other instances in the network. The usage of ZMQ certificates for these communications makes it so that only trustworthy rules are propagated through the network and deployed onto the hosts.

With our new JDS, clusters now build the workers' images at startup, which makes it a little slower that a Briareos cluster startup, and the broker now displays when a packet was dropped by a worker. The broker now offloads tasks to workers based on the captured packet, as shown in Listing 5.4 and complemented by Listing 6.22, instead of simply based on a LRU queue. Worker instances also now process packets much faster than their Briareos counterparts, as the results obtained by their engines' processing are on-par with the results obtained by the JHCs' engines'.

8.1   Future work

In the future, automatic updates to the .jar files, as well as to the configurations files, should be added, so that it becomes less of a hassle for an administrator to work with multiple JHCs and clusters. There should also be less reliance on external libraries such as NEMO's, so as to maintain JBriareos independent from other projects. Secure communications were only implemented to and from the JMS, as it was assumed that communications with the JDS are always secure. Secure communications between JHCs and the broker, and among other JDS components could also be implemented. It is also possible to store rules created by JHCs on disk, in cases where that host does not have a connection to the JMS. In that manner, those rules can then be uploaded to the JMS whenever a connection is able to be established between both parties.

Comparisons between our system and other more widespread solutions such as those described in chapter 2 should also be performed, in order to better place JBriareos among other systems. The migration of this project to lower-level programming languages such as C++, Rust or Go, so as to improve performance even further, should also be considered.

As it stands, the JMS is a single point of failure, as in if it fails, rules and pipeline configurations are not able to be shared nor deployed. To tackle this issue, the JMS could be replicated between N nodes, and a consensus algorithm implemented, so that it becomes more fault tolerant.

Finally and more importantly, JBriareos could make use of MISP [51] [52] to send and receive intelligence about possible threats and vulnerabilities, being both integrated with it by exporting information about uncovered threats and importing it from MISP to complement our own information sharing network.